Fat Quarter
PATCHWORK QUILTS

12 Beginner Patterns to Make with Precut Bundles

Stephanie Soebbing

Landauer Publishing

Fat Quarter Patchwork Quilts

Landauer Publishing (*www.landauerpub.com*) is an imprint of Fox Chapel Publishing Company, Inc.

Copyright © 2021 by Stephanie Soebbing and Fox Chapel Publishing Company, Inc. 903 Square Street, Mount Joy, PA 17552.

Project Team
Editor: Amy Deputato
Copy Editor: Hayley DeBerard
Designer: Wendy Reynolds
Photographers: Mike Mihalo Photography, 6, 7, 12 (bottom), 13 (bottom), 15 (bottom right), 17 (top right), 18, 21, 23, 27, 33, 39, 40, 45, 47, 51, 55, 61, 67, 72, 77, 83, 89; Stephanie Soebbing, all photos not otherwise credited
Illustrations pages 19–23 by Sue Friend

ISBN: 978-1-947163-80-5

Library of Congress Control Number: 2021940900

We are always looking for talented authors. To submit an idea, please send a brief inquiry to acquisitions@foxchapelpublishing.com.

Printed in Singapore

24 23 22 21   2 4 6 8 10 9 7 5 3 1

This book has been published with the intent to provide accurate and authoritative information in regard to the subject matter within. While every precaution has been taken in the preparation of this book, the author and publisher expressly disclaim any responsibility for any errors, omissions, or adverse effects arising from the use or application of the information contained herein.

Contents

Introduction

My infatuation with fat quarters started very early on in my quilting life. I got so much joy from collecting little bits of fabric that I fell in love with at the quilt shop. At first, I would collect fabrics according to color or theme. I'd fold all the pieces to a uniform size and store them in baskets in my sewing room, where they would look lovely on my shelves, until I felt I had enough to make a quilt. Then, eventually, I started buying fat quarter bundles when I found a collection I loved.

Now, as a quilt pattern designer and quilt shop owner, one of my favorite parts of my work is being handed a stack of fat quarters for our subscription club, Stashin' with Stephanie. I hand-pick each collection, but it is months between when I order and when the fabric arrives, so it is always exciting to see and touch all the beautiful designs for the first time.

I stare at the fat quarters for a few days, letting the colors and designs marinate in my subconscious until they tell me what they would like to become. And that's how the quilts in this book came to be. They are a collection of designs that I mulled over and created to bring out the best parts of the fabric, so your stash can look just as pretty in the quilt as it does on display in your sewing room.

There are quilts with large pieces to show off those too-pretty-to-cut-up prints. There are quilts that play on light, medium, and dark color values to use your entire bundle or stash to its greatest potential. There are quilts that are so fast and easy that you can get them together in a weekend, and there are quilts that will challenge and stretch you as you line up triangle points.

No matter which quilt you choose, we have a free step-by-step video tutorial to go with it on our website (*quiltaddictsanonymous.com/tutorials*). We show you everything you need to know to make these quilts beautifully, no matter your skill level.

I hope this book inspires you to raid your stash to create color combinations that will look fabulous in these designs! Or maybe you'll tear into that fat quarter bundle that has been tied up on your shelf for years or grab a new one from a designer you just love.

My advice is to splurge on one background fabric rather than going scrappy. Negative space is important. By sticking with one background fabric, you give the eye a place to rest, and that lets your favorite fabric and the design shine. Now let's get started!

Happy quilting,
Stephanie Soebbing

Before You Begin

I use all my pattern-design go-tos—strip piecing, making triangles from squares, and fusible appliqué—to make the quilting process as simple and streamlined as possible, so that you can create these quilts and convince your friends that you spent hours and hours piecing the perfect quilt top! It'll be our little secret. (Well, everyone else who bought this book will know, but they'll keep quiet, too!) We'll also cover fabric selection and quilting decisions in each pattern, because those components can make or break a design.

Principles of Modern Design

There is no one way to define modern quilting. What is modern to one quilter leans toward traditional to another. Still, there are a few design elements that are consistent across many modern quilt designs: alternative grid, embracing minimalism, and modernizing traditional blocks, and expansive negative space.

Alternative Grid

Simply put, alternative grid means that you break the traditional grid structure of a quilt design, in which you make a specific number of blocks and sew them together in rows, with or without sashing and a border. It can be as simple as changing the focus from the center of the quilt to a corner or a side of the quilt. By shifting the focus from the traditional center, the quilt becomes more modern in design and appearance.

As a new quilter, I fell in love with the process of turning tiny pieces into something more beautiful than any of the parts alone. But the reproductions and florals never really fit with my modern style until I found contemporary fabrics and designs. Then I had pieces that I loved not only creating but also decorating my home with.

Ray of Sunshine (page 72) is a great example of eliminating the traditional block structure so that the visual interest shifts to the fabric choice and placement.

You also can do away with the block structure altogether, like in Sonic Boom (page 26). There is no "block," just 60-degree diamonds sewn together into diagonal rows to create six wedges that make up the final quilt. The visual interest is created by fabric choice and placement rather than by a complicated block design.

Embracing Minimalism

Despite having a lot going on in the fabric print, Strata (page 76) is an example of a minimalist quilt. The rows are made up of a combination of uniformly strip-pieced blocks and one big rectangle strip. It's really very simple, but the bold, modern fabrics make it pop. Color selection, fabric choice, and simple piecing all contribute to the minimal look of a quilt.

Modernizing Traditional Blocks

Using fun, modern prints in traditional quilt blocks is a great way to update the look of your quilt. In Cross & Dot (page 44), I used a bold, contemporary bird and butterfly print to make an otherwise traditional block look modern. Think about your favorite quilt block and how you can give it a makeover so it will fit in with the decor of today's trendiest home.

The simple rectangular shapes and bold fabrics in Strata (page 76) are what make this quilt look modern.

You can't get much more traditional than a star block. Cross & Dot (page 44) uses the very traditional star made from a combination of squares, rectangles, and flying geese, but the modern, whimsical fabric choice is what brings this quilt into the twenty-first century.

Expansive Negative Space

Many modern quilts make use of large areas of negative space. This helps emphasize the parts of the quilt that are meant to shine through intricate piecing, design, or fabric selection, and it provides a fabulous canvas for quilting.

Essential Tools

If you are just starting out, there are "must-have" tools, and then there are the additional tools that will make your projects come together faster and easier. Here are some of the essentials you want to consider before getting started, as well as what they do and why you might want to try them.

Sewing machine

Thread

Sewing Machine

This may seem like a no-brainer, but a machine is the first and most important tool you will need to learn how to quilt. You don't need anything fancy to start. As long as it will sew a straight stitch and is clean, you'll be fine.

If you do purchase a new machine, I recommend buying one from a local store where you can learn how to use it and they will service it for you.

Quarter-Inch Presser Foot

Every quilt pattern I've ever read is written for a ¼" (0.64cm) seam allowance. The easiest way to maintain a consistent seam is to use a ¼" (0.64cm) presser foot. Some feet maintain this measurement when the needle is centered and the seam is sewn along the outer edge of the foot. Other types have a small metal guide to move your fabric along when you are sewing a seam. Machines might come with a dedicated ¼" (0.64cm) foot, or you can purchase one of the available after-market feet.

Walking Foot

Use a walking foot any time you are moving three or more layers through your sewing machine. The walking foot is special because it has small ridges, or "feed dogs," on top of the foot that move in tandem with the feed dogs under the throat plate of your machine. Layers are moved through the machine at the same rate, preventing bunching or puckering.

Thread

Choosing a good thread can prevent headaches as you sew. Quality thread can help avoid lint build-up, extending the time you can go between cleanings. Also, when you move from piecing to quilting, thread choice plays a powerful role in the finished look of the quilt.

For piecing and quilting on my home sewing machine, I use Aurifil™ 50wt thread. I like to piece with white thread no matter what color of fabric I'm working with, and I use all colors of thread for quilting.

Rotary Cutters

To the untrained eye, a rotary cutter looks and works like a pizza cutter. A rotary cutter allows you to cut fabric quickly, easily, and accurately with the aid of an acrylic ruler or template. There are many options on the market, but they all do the same thing. A rotary cutter's blade is very sharp, and it can cut quickly and unexpectedly if you aren't careful with it. Always make sure your blade is in the safety setting when you aren't using your rotary cutter.

Cutting Mats

I suggest you buy no smaller than an 18" x 24" (45.72 x 60.96cm) self-healing cutting mat. With that size or larger, you'll be able to cut strips across the width of fabric (WOF), which is required for nearly every pattern in this book. Mats are gridded to assist you in cutting, but it's important to make sure the 1" (2.54cm) squares of the grid are accurate.

Quilting Rulers

Acrylic quilting rulers come in all shapes and sizes, but the 6" x 24" (15.24 x 60.96cm) ruler is one of the most versatile. This ruler spans the width of the folded fabric and can be used to cut strips, squares, and even triangles. Try to find a ruler with 30-, 45-, and 60-degree lines on it so you can also use it to trim triangle blocks. For smaller cuts, try a 6½" (16.51cm) square ruler for cutting, trimming, and squaring up pieces.

Pins

You need something to hold your fabric together as you sew, and pins are that something! I prefer flower-head pins because they slide easily into quilting fabric, they're easy to grab, and they're cute! Try to find long, thin pins for easier handling.

Rotary cutters

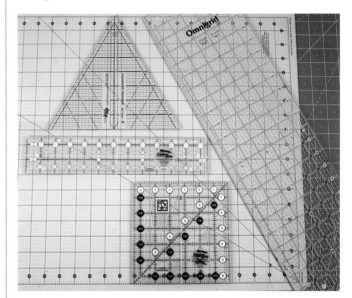

Quilting rulers

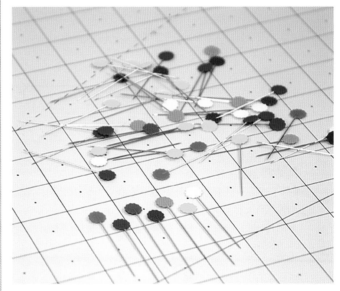

Flower-head pins

Quilting Fabric

When you start quilting, buy the best fabric you can afford. It will be well worth it in the end. Quilt-shop quality cotton is always worth the money because the thread count is higher, the fabric holds its shape, and it's usually softer.

To choose your fabric, start by finding a focal print that you love, then pick supporting prints that complement the focal fabric. One great way to find coordinating colors is to choose prints from one fabric line. Most lines have twelve to twenty-four coordinating prints, so you can't go wrong.

When I'm planning a scrappy quilt, I often choose two colors and raid my stash for fabrics that work in that theme. (Of course, if you're just starting to quilt, you may not have this option.) I recommend buying a neutral to tie them all together. Neutral doesn't mean white or tan. One of the quilts in this book uses pink as a neutral.

There is a great debate on whether to prewash your fabric. I never prewash my fabric because the combination of shrinkage and frayed edges often make the piece too small to get all the pieces you need out of it. As long as you purchase quilt-shop quality cotton, your fabric will shrink evenly when you wash your completed quilt the first time, and you won't have to worry about the colors bleeding—although it is a good idea to throw a color-catcher laundry sheet (or three) in the wash with the quilt the first time you wash it, just in case.

Quilting fabric

Batting

Batting is the layer that goes in between the quilt top and backing fabric. It provides warmth and creates texture to the top when quilted. I prefer Quilters Dream® batting and alternate between 100% cotton and 80/20 cotton/poly blend. Natural fibers help the cotton quilting fabric stick to the batting, making it easier to keep the fabric from bunching, especially if you are quilting on your home machine.

Another consideration for batting is color. It comes in natural, white, and black. I use white batting if there are white or gray neutrals in my quilt. I like the look of

bleached white batting behind these colors. When I am working with a very dark or black background, I opt for black polyester batting. Occasionally bits of batting will get pushed through the quilting stitches, and if you use black batting, you will never see it.

Perfect Piecing

There are two skills you need to master to create perfect piecing. Accurate cutting is the first, followed by sewing an accurate ¼" (0.64cm) seam. Quilting fabric comes from the store folded in half with the selvages touching. The selvage is the edge on each side of the fabric that prevents it from unraveling. Leave your fabric folded when you start. You will need to straighten the edge that was cut from the bolt, as starting with a straight fabric edge will guarantee accurate cuts.

Straightening the Fabric and Cutting Strips

1. Lay the fabric on a cutting mat with the cut side toward the right side of the mat. Smooth out any wrinkles. With the fold at the bottom of the mat, place a 6" x 24" (15.24 x 60.96cm) ruler on the fabric so that it spans the entire WOF. Align the ruler so the 1" (2.54cm) line is even with the fold of the fabric. Extend the fabric beyond the ruler's edge, just enough to straighten the fabric.

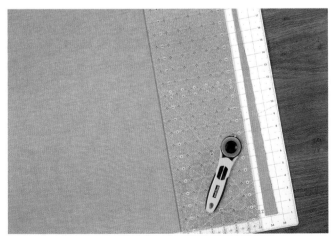

2. Hold the ruler down firmly with the palm of your hand and use a rotary cutter to cut along the ruler's edge.

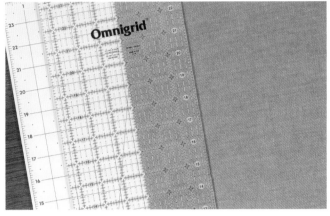

3. Flip the fabric to the left side of the cutting mat and realign the ruler on the 1" (2.54cm) line. For example, we're cutting a 3" (7.62cm) strip. Align the 3" (7.62cm) line of the ruler along the straightened edge of the fabric. Repeat Step 2 and cut the strip.

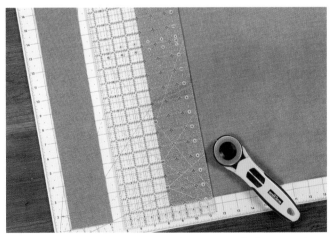

4. Continue cutting strips in this manner. As long as the 1" (2.54cm) line of the ruler is on the fabric fold, and the line of the required strip width aligns along the edge of the fabric, you will have straight, accurate strips. If you are cutting a lot of strips, it's a good idea to occasionally check the fabric edge to make sure it's still straight. Check by repeating Step 1.

Cutting Diamonds

I use the Clearview Triangle™ for all the diamond cuts in this book. Some rulers have blunt tips, but the Clearview has three points intact. **Note:** Yardage requirements are based on the use of this ruler, so it's important to use a ruler with three sharp points for your project. The following step-by-step instructions are for cutting diamonds for quilts like Sparkle (page 82). Regardless of the strip size, the instructions for lining up the ruler are the same for any size diamond you want to cut. Refer to the specific quilt instructions for strip size.

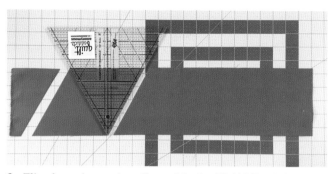

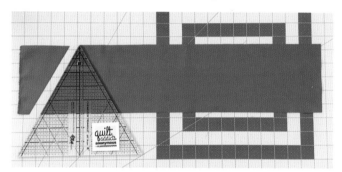

1. On a 5" (12.7cm) x WOF strip, line up the Clearview Triangle ruler on the 5" (12.7cm) line of the ruler. The top and bottom of the ruler should align with the top and bottom of the strip as shown above. Cut off the corner and discard.

2. Flip the ruler and realign with the 5" (12.7cm) line on top of the strip and the point aligned with the corner of the fabric as shown above. Cut along the right side of the ruler to create a diamond.

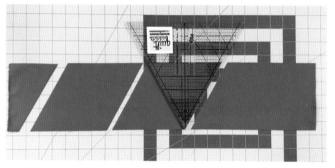

3. There is no need to flip the ruler for cuts. Move it along the fabric strip, realigning as you cut.

Using these instructions for cutting the fabric in the Sonic Boom (page 26), Bling (page 38), Sparkle (shown here and page 82), and Stargazer (page 88) quilts will make cutting all those diamonds much easier and quicker.

Cutting Triangles

These step-by-step instructions demonstrate how to cut triangles for quilts like Bling (page 38), Lily Field (page 60), Rainbow Frosting (page 66), Sparkle (82), and Stargazer (page 88). The instructions are the same for any size triangle you want to cut.

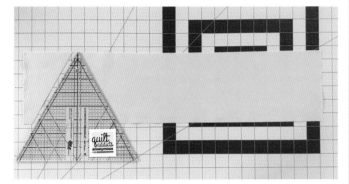

1. On a 5¼" (13.34cm) x WOF strip, line up the 60-degree triangle ruler on the 5¼" (13.34cm) line, ¼" (0.64cm) away from the edge as shown above. Cut off the corner and reserve the half-triangles.

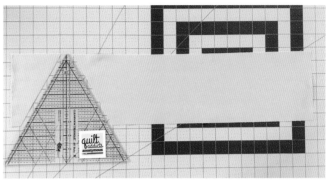

2. With the ruler in place, cut along the right side of the ruler to create a triangle.

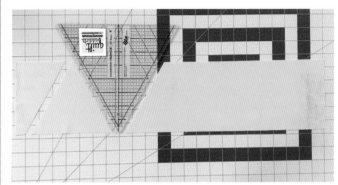

3. Flip the ruler back and forth, realigning and cutting triangles as you move across the strip of fabric.

Rainbow Frosting (page 66) is made up entirely of equilateral triangles.

Sewing a Seam

The other skill needed for perfect piecing is sewing an accurate ¼" (0.64cm) seam. Not all ¼" (0.64cm) feet are identical because manufacturers make them specifically for their own sewing machines. If your machine comes with one, that's great. If not, you'll still be able to sew a perfect seam without one.

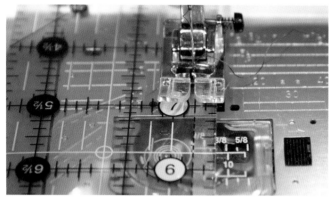

1. With the needle aligned on the ¼" (0.64cm) line of a ruler, check to see where the edge of your presser foot falls. You can see that this foot won't sew a ¼" (0.64cm) seam.

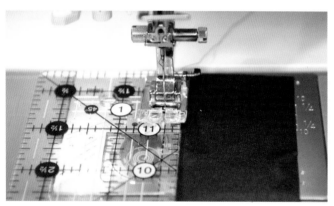

2. Take a piece of tape and lay it against the edge of the ruler, pressing the tape down on the throat of your machine. Use the edge of the tape as your ¼" (0.64cm) guide.

Pro Tip

Some patterns tell you to sew a scant ¼" (0.64cm) seam, for instance, when making half-square triangles. When a half-square triangle is folded open at the seam, it actually takes up a couple of threads. By sewing a couple of threads short of the ¼" (0.64cm), you will maintain the correct size of your half-square triangle.

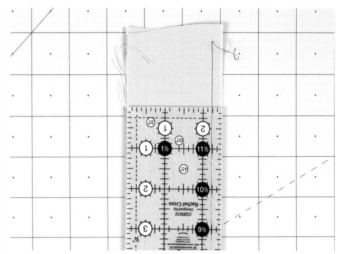

3. However you choose to sew your seam, it's a good idea to check it for accuracy. An extra ⅛" (0.32cm) may not seem like a lot, but those eighths can add up quickly, and you may end up with pieces that do not fit together.

Strip Piecing

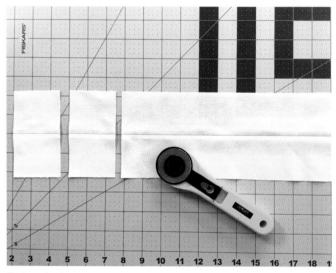

Strip piecing is a great way to speed up your quilting. Layer two strips with right sides together, then sew along one end until you reach the edge of the fabric. Grab the next set of strips to be sewn together and layer them right sides together. Lift the presser foot up and slide the next set in, leaving a little space between it and the set you just finished sewing. Continue adding pieces in this manner until you have a set of multiple strips.

Half-Square Triangles

There are many ways to sew half-square triangles, but my favorite way is to make them from squares. I can get two-for-one triangles, and it's easier than sewing individual triangles on the bias because it avoids fabric stretch. I use this technique in the En Pointe (page 50), Geometric Garden (page 54), and Ray of Sunshine (page 72) quilts.

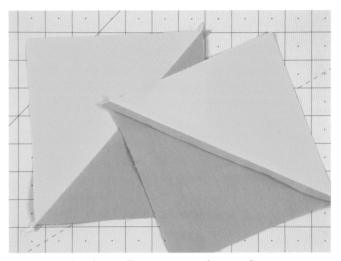

3. Cut on the drawn line, open, and press the seams.

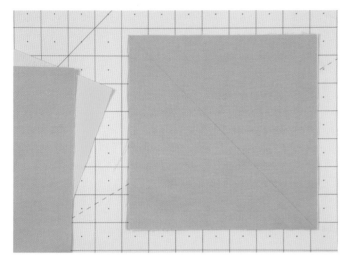

1. Draw a diagonal line from corner to corner on the wrong side of a square. Layer the right sides together with a second square.

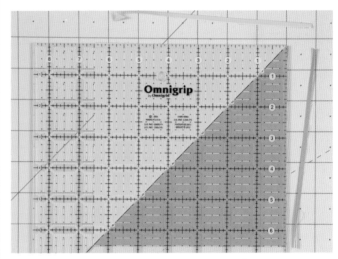

4. Square up the half-square triangles to the measurement in the project.

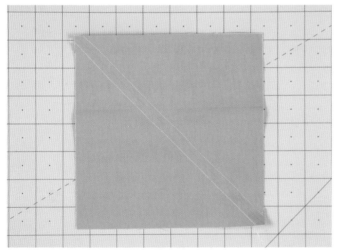

2. Sew a scant ¼" (0.64cm) seam on either side of the drawn line.

Ray of Sunshine (page 72) is made entirely of half-square triangles.

Diamonds and Equilateral Triangles

All equilateral triangles and diamonds in this book are cut using the Clearview Triangle ruler. I find the 8" (20.32cm) version the most versatile. With three sharp points, the ruler makes it easy for me to line up my pieces quickly, pin, and sew. The fabric ears are called "dog ears," and they become a good reference as you align the pieces.

Triangles and diamonds are sewn in diagonal rows, which takes away the need to sew dreaded Y-seams. Because the pieces are cut on the bias, the seams can be stretchy, so it's important to pin pieces together and not pull, push, or stretch the fabric as it goes through your machine. I like to use a double-pinning method on all my 60-degree quilts to ensure that the points come together perfectly. I show this method in all the video tutorials for the quilts in this book (*QuiltAddictsAnonymous.com/ tutorials*) so you can watch how I get everything lined up.

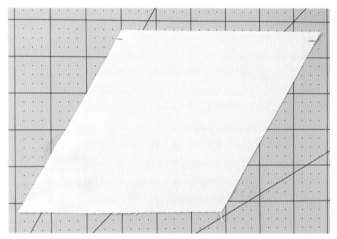

1. Align the ¼" (0.64cm) mark of a ruler along the edge of the diamond shape. With a removable marking tool, draw a small line at both points to mark the seam line.

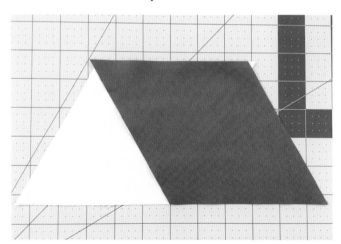

2. Layer a second diamond, right sides together. Align the ¼" (0.64cm) marks with edge of the second piece. The dog ears should extend ¼" (0.64cm) beyond the edge of the fabric as shown above.

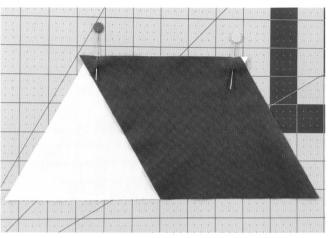

3. Pin the pieces at each point of the diamond and sew with a ¼" (0.64cm) seam. The seam should intersect in the valleys formed by the offset of the dog ears.

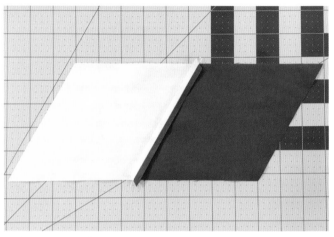

4. Press open the seams of the triangles and diamonds to make the quilt top lay flat.

The Quilt Sandwich

The first time I heard the term "quilt sandwich," I just nodded my head and pretended I knew what it meant. It was one of the strangest terms I'd ever heard! Eventually, I learned that it describes layering the quilt backing, batting, and quilt top. Making your quilt sandwich correctly is very critical to the outcome of your quilt.

Prepping the Quilt Top

Before layering the quilt top, carefully press it and then sew a ⅛" (0.32cm) seam around the entire perimeter. The stitching acts like a stay stitch, ensuring that the edges of the quilt stay square and straight before quilting. It also helps hold sewn seams together while quilting.

Prepping the Backing

Backing fabric should always measure 10" (25.40cm) wider than the quilt top to allow for shrinkage as you quilt. After quilting, you will trim any excess. You will piece the backing, or you may find 108" (2.7m) fabric at a quilt shop to accommodate a seamless backing on your quilt. Fabric requirements that include extra fabric for backing are included in the materials lists of the projects in this book.

To prep your backing fabric, cut off selvages with a rotary cutter. Cut the backing fabric into as many equal widths as you need to span the quilt. With right sides together, sew the widths of fabric together along the cut sides, using a ¼" (0.64cm) seam. Press the seams open and press the backing fabric well.

Choosing your backing fabric is a lot of fun. You can choose a fun printed fabric (Rainbow Frosting, page 66) or a plain colored fabric (Sonic Boom, page 26).

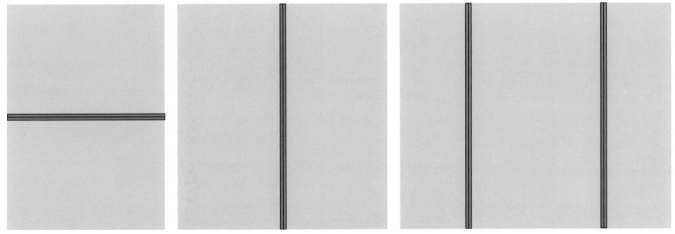

Quilt backing is sewn together from widths of fabric with the seams running either horizontally (left) or vertically (center). Quilts smaller than 74" (187.96cm) on any side will use two widths of fabric sewn together to make the backing. Quilts larger than 74" (187.96cm) will require three widths of fabric (right) sewn together to create a backing large enough to extend 10" (25.4cm) larger than the quilt top.

Layering the Quilt Sandwich

You will need a large, flat area to lay out your backing, batting, and quilt top; the size of this area depends on the size of your quilt. I created my work surface out of a pair of 6' (1.8m) tables and two sets of plastic bed risers. I placed the tables side by side on top of the risers to raise the tables to counter height. Layers don't have to fit edge to edge on the surface. They can drape evenly off the sides of a table.

Start by laying the backing wrong side up on your work surface and smoothing out any wrinkles. Use tape or binder clips to keep the backing in place.

Layer the bumpy side of the batting, facing up, on the quilt backing. Smooth out any wrinkles. (**Note:** If wrinkles are hard to smooth out, throw the batting in the dryer on low heat with a wet washcloth for a few minutes to reduce wrinkles.) Then center the quilt top over the backing and batting, making sure to smooth out all three layers as much as possible.

Pinning the Quilt Sandwich

If you are quilting on your home sewing machine, I recommend pin-basting because it's the easiest way to keep layers in place. I prefer using bent quilting pins to make it easier to rock into and out of the layers. Start

in the center of the quilt and pin every 6" (15.25cm), through all three layers. Continue pinning, pulling the draped areas onto the table, and smoothing out the layers. (**Note:** If you are using your dining-room table or anything other than a dedicated work surface, take care not to poke pins into the surface.)

Quilting the Quilt

The process of quilting a quilt can and does merit its own book. I suggest that you first make some small quilt sandwiches and practice stitching. When you are comfortable, start quilting your project.

Straight-line quilting can be accomplished on your home machine using a walking foot. It always looks good and can be either simple or incredibly complex. I teach first-time quilters to sew straight lines about 2" (5.08cm) apart to secure the quilt layers. It creates a pleasing design, and it's easy and functional at the same time. Quilt horizontally, vertically, or diagonally to create visual interest. You can create amazing texture by quilting very densely. You can also use quilting stencils to mark complicated free-motion quilting designs so that you have a line to follow to create beautiful designs.

Choosing a quilt design is as much of a creative decision as choosing your fabrics and pattern design. Whether you choose a simple design or a more intricate one, quilting enhances the design of your project.

Finishing the Quilt

Binding the Quilt

Congratulations! You've pieced your top, you've quilted, and now it is time to bind. Binding is the piece of fabric that wraps around the raw edges of your quilt to hide the batting and secure the edges of your quilt. I always write my patterns to include 2½" (6.40cm) binding.

My preferred method of sewing binding is the continuous method, so that you can't tell where the binding strip starts and stops. It makes a nice, smooth finish around all the edges. Joining the ends can be a little intimidating at first, but once you do it, you'll never want to go back to methods that tuck the strip and create a lump. The Quilt Addicts Anonymous Beginner Quilting series at *quiltaddictsanonymous.com* includes a free video that shows you each of the steps explained in this section.

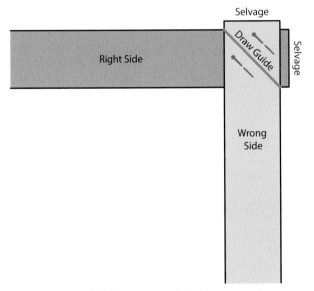

1. Arrange your binding strips right sides together at a right angle so that the horizontal strip is right side up and the vertical strip is right side down. Allow the selvages to hang past the edges of the strips. This will create two valleys that you will sew between. Pin the strips in place. Draw a line from valley to valley from the top left to the bottom right.

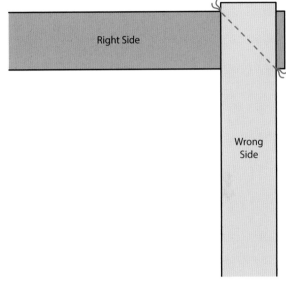

2. Sew on the line, removing the pins before you sew over them.

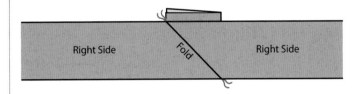

3. Open your strip to make sure the two strips make a straight line.

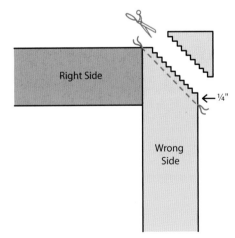

4. Trim the corner off to create a ¼" (0.64cm) seam. Repeat until all your binding strips are sewn together.

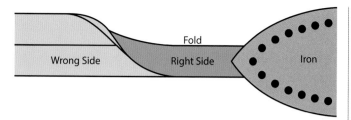

5. Fold the binding in half with the long sides together and press in place. Press diagonal seams to the side as you come to them.

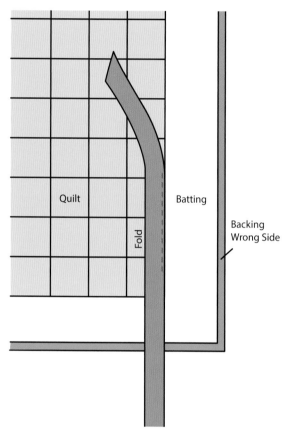

6. Starting on the bottom of your quilt, lay your binding even with the edge of your quilt top. Leave about 6" (15.24cm) free and start sewing the binding to the edge of your quilt top through all three layers using a walking foot, keeping the edges of the binding even with the edge of the quilt top at all times. I use Machingers® Quilting Gloves at this step to help grip the fabric and move the quilt through the machine easily.

7. Stop with your needle down when you are ¼" (0.64cm) away from the edge of the first corner. Lift your presser foot and turn the quilt so that the next edge is now facing you. Lift your needle up and gently pull the quilt out from under the presser foot a couple of inches (about 5cm).

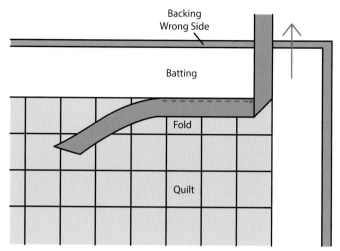

8. Fold the binding back so that the raw edges are even with the side of the quilt top and the fold makes a 45-degree angle directly into the corner of the quilt.

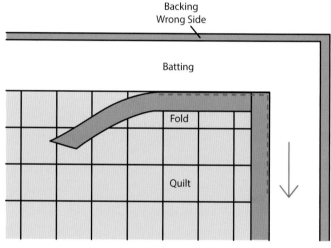

9. Fold the binding down so that the raw edges are even with the edges of the quilt top and there is a triangle flap at the corner. You will turn this flap over the quilt corner and stitch it down later to create a mitered corner.

10. Continue sewing, repeating the mitered corner steps for the remaining three corners. Stop sewing about 12" (30.48cm) before the point where you started sewing. Break your thread and remove the quilt from the sewing machine.

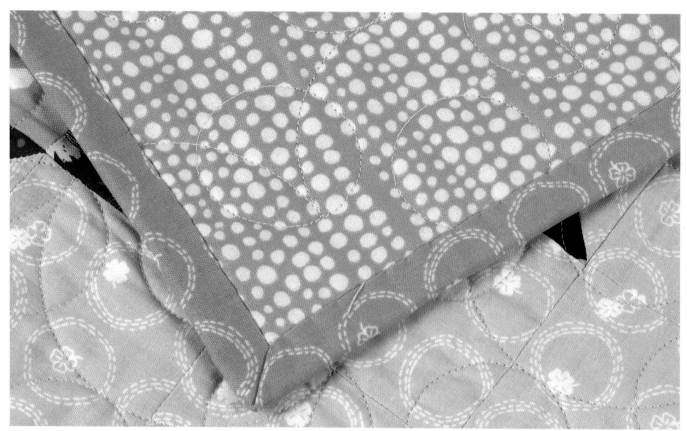

Stitching the binding to the back of the quilt by hand takes a bit more time, but the results are worth it. Grab a needle, thimble, and thread and start binging a new show while you work.

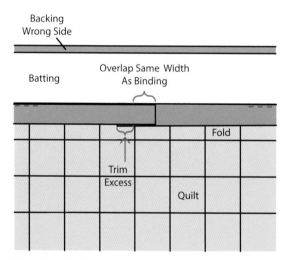

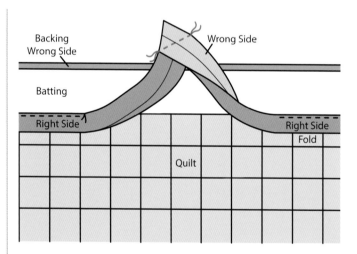

11. Select the beginning of the binding and trim it square in the center of the open section of binding. This should be about 6" (15.24cm) in between where the binding starts and stops. Lay the quilt flat on a table and arrange the trimmed binding piece flat against it with the raw edges of the binding even with the edges of the quilt top. Lay a ruler even with the trimmed edge of the binding. Now lay the end of the binding over the beginning of the binding, keeping the raw edges even with the edges of the quilt. Trim the binding end so that it overlaps exactly 2½" (6.35cm) past the beginning of the binding.

12. Arrange the binding edges perpendicular to each other like you did when first sewed the binding strips together, except now the edges will lines up exactly. Pin them in place and draw a line from the corners of the binding so that you have a guide to sew on. Sew the binding together, removing the pins before you sew over them.

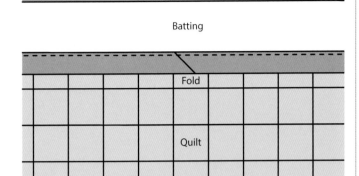

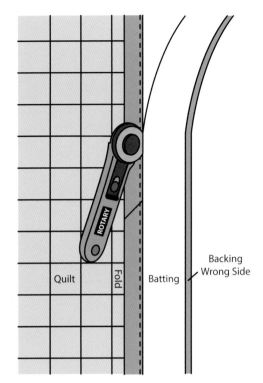

13. Lay the quilt back on a flat table and test to make sure the binding lies flat against the quilt top with no excess fabric or tightness. Once you are satisfied, trim the seam to ¼" (0.64cm) and sew the binding to the quilt top through all three layers.

Stitching Tips

- When you stitch your binding down by hand, it is important that your stitches are not seen from the front of the quilt. To do this, insert your needle into the quilt backing and batting, but not through the top, right below where your needle came out of the binding fold. Travel into the quilt batting about ¼" (0.64cm) over and bring the needle out on the fold of the binding. Repeat this blind stitch until you reach the corner of the quilt.

- When you need to tie off a piece of thread, place the knot within one or two stitches from the stitch you just made. Then take another stitch and bury your knot by traveling with your needle about 1" (2.54cm) and tugging the knot in between the layers of the quilt. When you start a new thread, start a couple of inches (about 5cm) behind where you just tied off to make a stronger seam.

- Binding clips to hold layers together and thread that matches your binding fabric can make binding much easier when you are just getting started.

14. Trim the excess batting off so that the batting and backing are now even with the quilt top. When trimming the mitered corners, be careful that you don't accidentally slice the binding.

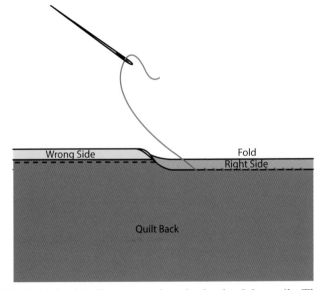

15. Fold the binding around to the back of the quilt. The binding should fit snugly around the edges of the quilt; there should be neither a gap between the edge of the batting and the edge of the binding nor a bump where the batting is folded back because the binding is folded too far. Knot your thread and insert your needle about 1" (2.54cm) from the edge of your binding, going through the quilt back and batting but not the top. Bring the needle out on the fold of the binding. Give your thread a tug to bury the knot in between the quilt layers. Blind stitch until you reach the corner of the quilt.

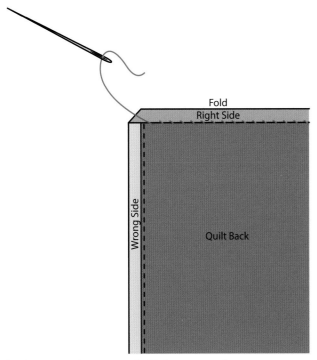

16. Once you have sewed all the way to the corner, use your needle to travel to the front corner of the quilt, bringing your needle out right where the binding makes a 45-degree fold on the front of your quilt. Insert your needle through the 45-degree fold, coming out in the back corner of the quilt. Fold the next binding edge down so that it makes a 45-degree angle and meets the edge of the edge you just finished sewing. Take two or three stitches down the 45-degree fold, tacking it down. Take one extra stitch at the bottom of the 45-degree fold and then continue with the blind stitch and mitered corners until the binding is complete.

Labeling Your Quilt

I always label each of my quilts, including my name and the year the quilt was finished. You can include additional information, such as to whom the quilt was gifted, the name of the pattern, and the occasion on which it was given. Future generations will appreciate this information.

You can buy commercial labels or make your own. Either embroider the details or use a permanent, colorfast pen to write the information. When you've completed this final touch, you have finished your quilt!

Whether you use commercial labels or decide to make your own, you should definitely label your quilts. Quilts are items that tend to stick with a family for generations, so having a label on a quilt will make it more personal and give it life.

Projects

Sonic Boom

Quilted by Shelly Moore

Sonic Boom is a celebration of color that is perfect for any rainbow fat quarter bundle. The offset bursting star gradually fades from one color to the next—from a bright orange in the center out to purple at the edges. I used fabric from the master of the rainbow, Tula Pink, with her Tula's True Colors collection for FreeSpirit Fabrics, but any rainbow collection or even gradated ombré would be fun.

This quilt does not contain a traditional quilt block, and it's not put together in regular rows, either, but it is simple and fast. You're going to cut your fat quarters into 60-degree diamonds and sew them into six wedges, then join the wedges to complete your quilt top. No dreaded Y-seams required!

Fabric Requirements

	Fat Quarters	Backing	Finished Size
Throw	19	3¾ yards (3.43m)	56⅜" x 56⅞" (1.43 x 1.44m)

Cutting Instructions

You must use a 60-degree triangle ruler with all three points, like the Clearview Triangle, in order to cut the right number of diamonds and triangles for this pattern. The cutting instructions will not work if you use a 60-degree triangle ruler with one blunt point.

FAT QUARTERS

1. From each fat quarter, cut three 5" x 21" (12.70 x 53.34cm) strips and one 2½" x 21" (6.35 x 53.34cm) strip. Set the 2½" x 21" (6.35 x 53.34cm) strip aside for scrappy binding.

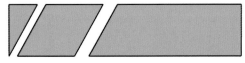

2. Select a 5" (12.70cm) strip. Using a 60-degree triangle ruler, line the 5" (12.70 cm) line up with the bottom of the strip and line up the point even with the top of the strip. Cut the corner off the strip, leaving a 60-degree angle on the edge of the strip. Discard the corner.

Flip the 60-degree ruler over so that the 5" (12.70 cm) line is even with the top of the strip and the point is even with the bottom of the strip. The left side of the ruler should be even with the top left point you just cut.

Cut along the right side of the ruler to create a 60-degree diamond.

Continue sliding the ruler down to cut three 5" (12.70cm) diamonds from each strip, for a total of nine 5" (12.70 cm) diamonds from each fat quarter.

Wedge Assembly Instructions

This quilt is actually quite easy. You just need to master sewing diamonds together, label your fabrics from 1 to 19 as they fade from one color to another in the color wheel, and pay attention to the color numbers as you sew.

We will start with basic instructions to sew the diamonds together. Then use these instructions to sew your rows together, making the quilt in a set of six wedges instead of traditional blocks. We're going to start with Wedge 2.

1. Select one diamond each from Fabrics 1, 2, 4, and 6. Arrange as shown above.

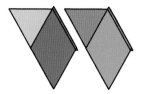

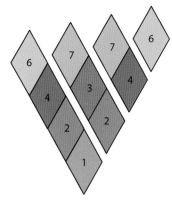

2. Flip the diamond from Fabric 4 down, so when the right sides are together with Fabric 6, the diamonds point in opposite directions, as seen above. The points will stick out on either side about ¼" (0.64cm). Do the same with Fabrics 1 and 2: flip Fabric 1 down, right sides together, with Fabric 2.

Sew Fabrics 4 and 6 together and Fabrics 1 and 2 together. Your ¼" (0.64cm) seam line should be right in the valley where the points meet, as indicated by the black seam line above.

6. Follow the process outlined in Steps 1–5 to complete the other rows in Wedge 2 as shown above. Pay careful attention to the fabric number placement when sewing the rows together.

3. Press the seams open. This is the beginning of the first row of Wedge 2.

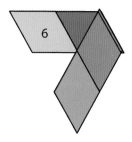

4. Flip the right side of the row right sides together with the left side of the row, with Fabrics 2 and 4 facing each other. The halves of the row will be pointing in opposite directions as shown above. The points will stick out on either side about ¼" (0.64cm).

Sew together with your ¼" (0.64cm) seam line right in the valley where the points meet, as indicated by the black seam line above.

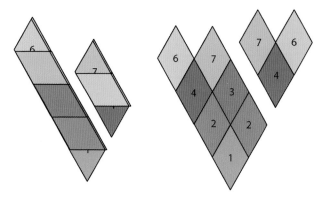

7. Flip the second row right sides together with the first row, and the fourth row right sides together with the third row, as shown above. Pin the seams to ensure that the diamond points match when you sew them together. The points at the row edges will stick out ¼" (0.64cm) as shown above. Sew a ¼" (0.64cm) seam.

8. Press the seams open.

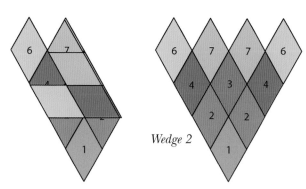

Wedge 2

5. Press the seam open to complete the row.

9. Repeat Steps 7 and 8 to sew the first and second rows to the third and fourth rows to complete Wedge 2.

10. Use the numbered diagrams on pages 29–30 to sew one of each wedge together. First, sew the diamonds into rows, then sew the rows together to make each wedge. Press all seams open.

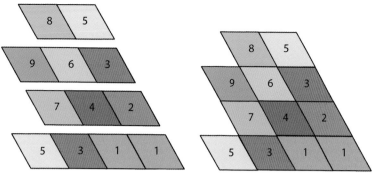

Wedge 1

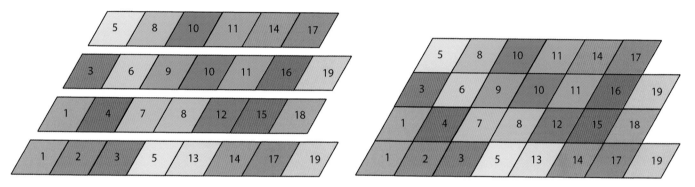

Wedge 3

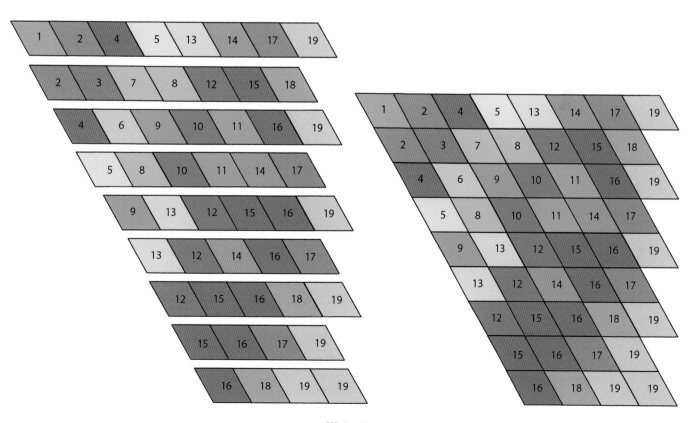

Wedge 4

Wedge 5

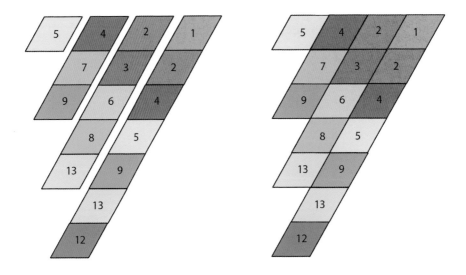

Wedge 6

Quilt Assembly Instructions

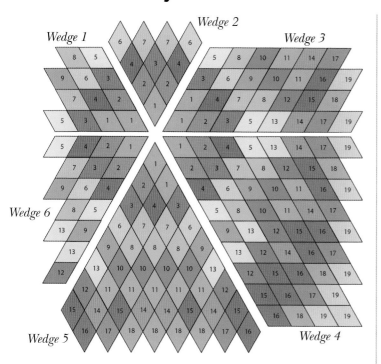

Quilt assembly diagram

1. Arrange the wedges as shown above in the quilt assembly diagram.

2. Sew Wedge 3 to Wedge 2 and press the seam open. Then sew Wedge 1 to Wedge 2, pressing the seam open to create the top half. Repeat with the bottom half, sewing Wedge 4 to Wedge 5 and pressing the seam open. Then sew Wedge 6 to Wedge 5, pressing the seam open to create the bottom half.

3. Sew the two halves together to form the quilt top.

Quilt layout diagram

4. Trim the quilt sides so that the edge is ¼" (0.64cm) beyond the point of the outer diamond tips.

5. Sew a ⅛" (0.32cm) stay-stitch around the edges of the quilt top to prevent the bias edges from stretching during the quilting process.

Dot Dash

Quilted by Shelly Moore

The inspiration for Dot Dash came from a really simple place. For every new collection we bring to Quilt Addicts Anonymous, we create a graphic collage to show off the beautiful fabrics online. The collage we created for Reverie by Shell Rummel for FreeSpirit Fabrics looked a lot like the final block design in Dot Dash. I just fell in love with how the simplistic nature of the collage surrounded by thin strips of white showed off the delicate watercolor prints of orchids and other bits of nature.

I framed the blocks using Karma Cotton by Valori Wells. Quilters often overlook using woven fabrics in quilts, but they work beautifully, add texture, and, in this case, add to the airiness of the design.

Fabric Requirements

	Fat Quarters	Background	Backing	# of Blocks	Finished Size
Crib	4	1¾ yards (1.60m)	1¾ yards (1.60m)	12	37" x 49" (0.94 x 1.24m)
Twin	12	3½ yards (3.20m)	5¼ yards (5.74m)	35	61" x 85" (1.55 x 2.16m)
Full	14	4 yards (3.66m)	5¼ yards (5.74m)	42	73" x 85" (1.85 x 2.16m)
King	22	5½ yards (5.03m)	9 yards (8.23m)	64	97" x 97" (2.46 x 2.46m)

Cutting Instructions

FAT QUARTERS

1. From half or two (six, seven, eleven) of the fat quarters, cut:
- Two 5½" x 21" (13.97 x 53.34cm) strips
- Two 2½" X 21" (6.35 x 53.34cm) strips

2. From half or two (six, seven, eleven) of the fat quarters, cut:
- One 5½" x 21" (15.97 x 53.34cm) strip
- Four 2½" x 21" (6.35 x 53.34cm) strips
- One 1½" x 21" (3.81 x 53.34cm) strip

BACKGROUND

3. Cut six (eighteen, twenty-one, thirty-two) 1½" (3.81cm) x WOF strips. Cross-cut each strip at the fold to create twelve (thirty-six, forty-two, sixty-four) 1½" x 21" (3.81 x 53.34cm) strips.

4. Cut two (four, five, seven) 11½" (29.21cm) x WOF strips. Cross-cut each strip into twenty-eight 1½" x 11½" (72.39 x 29.21cm) rectangles, for a total of thirty-six (105, 126, 192).

5. Cut one (two, two, three) more 11½" (29.21cm) x WOF strips. Cross-cut each at the fold to create two 11½" x 21" (3.81 x 53.34cm) rectangles, for a total of two, (four, four, six).

6. Cut five (eight, nine, ten) 2½" (6.35cm) x WOF strips for binding.

Note: If you are working with more than one colorway, you may want to organize your strips by color, but feel free to mix and match.

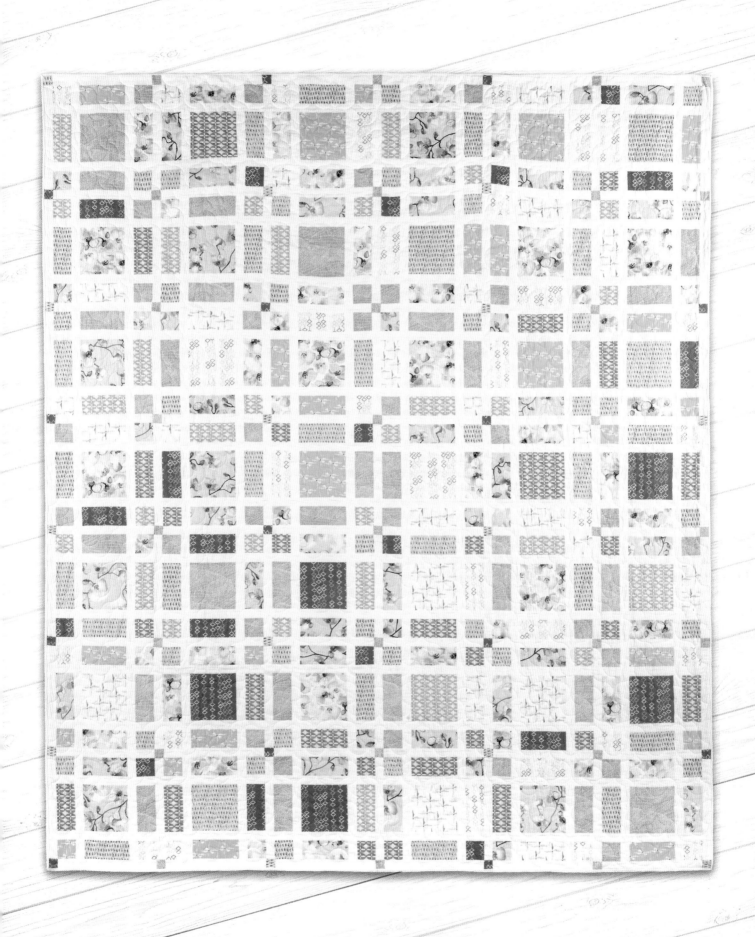

Block Assembly Instructions

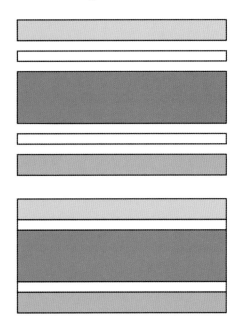

1. Select twelve (thirty-six, forty-two, sixty-four) 2½" x 21" (6.35 x 53.34cm) fat quarter strips, six (eighteen, twenty-one, thirty-two) 5½" x 21" (15.97 x 53.34cm) fat quarter strips, and twelve (thirty-six, forty-two, sixty-four) 1½" x 21" (3.81 x 53.34cm) background strips. Sew strips together along the long side to create an 11½" x 21" (29.21 x 53.34cm) strip-pieced unit. Press the seams open.

You will need six (eighteen, twenty-one, thirty-two) strip-pieced units.

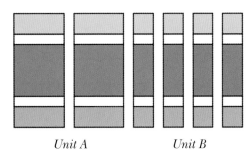

Unit A   *Unit B*

2. Cut each strip-pieced unit into:
- Two 5½" x 11½" (15.97 x 29.21cm) Unit A pieces; you will need twelve (thirty-five, forty-two, sixty-four)
- Four 2½" x 11½" (6.35 x 29.21cm) Unit B pieces; you will need twenty-four (seventy, eighty-four, 128)

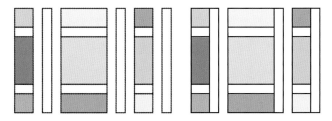

3. Select one Unit A, two Unit Bs, and three 1½" x 11½" (3.81 x 29.21cm) background rectangles. Arrange as shown, above left. Sew 1½" x 11½" (3.81 x 29.21cm) background strips to the right side of the Unit A and Unit B pieces. Press the seams open.

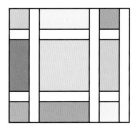

Unit C

4. Join Unit A and Unit B pieces as shown to create Unit C. Press the seams open. Unit C should measure 11½" (29.21cm) tall x 12½" (31.75cm) wide.

5. Repeat Steps 3–5 to create a total of twelve (thirty-five, forty-two, sixty-four) blocks.

6. Select two (four, four, six) 11½" x 21" (29.21 x 53.34cm) rectangles and two (four, four, six) 1½" x 21" (3.81 x 53.34cm) rectangles. Sew one of each strip together along the long side to create a 12½" x 21" (31.75 x 53.34cm) strip-pieced unit. Press the seams open. Create a total of two (four, four, six).

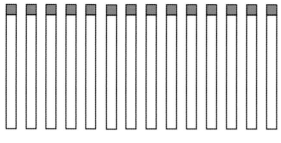

Unit D

7. Cross-cut each 12½" x 21" (31.75 x 53.34cm) strip-pieced unit into fourteen 1½" x 12½" (36.83 x 31.75cm) Unit D pieces—you will need twenty (forty-eight, fifty-six, eighty-one).

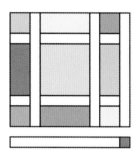 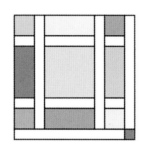

8. Select one Unit C and one Unit D and arrange as shown above. Sew together, pressing the seams open. Blocks will measure 12½" (31.75cm) square. Repeat to make a total of twelve (thirty-five, forty-two, sixty-four) blocks.

Quilt Assembly Instructions

1. Arrange blocks into a design that is pleasing to you according to the quilt layout diagram on page 37.

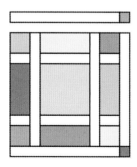 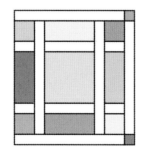

2. Once you determine which blocks will be in the top row, sew a Unit D piece to the top of two (four, five, seven) of the blocks in the top row, leaving out the block in the top left corner. Press the seams open.

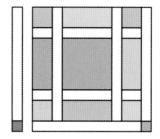 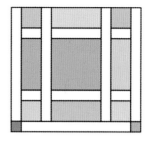

3. Sew a Unit D piece to the left side of three (six, six, seven) blocks in the first column on the left, leaving out the one in the top left corner. Press the seams open.

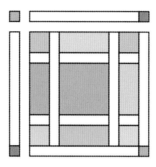

4. Use a seam ripper to remove a 1½" (3.81cm) square from an extra Unit D piece. Arrange it as shown above with two Unit D pieces and the block in the top left corner of the quilt. Sew the Unit D piece to the left side of the block and the 1½" (3.81cm) fat quarter square piece to the Unit D on the top row. Press the seams open.

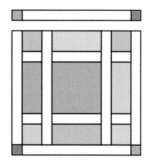 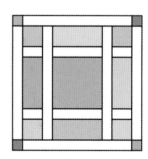

5. Join the top row to the block. Press the seam open.

6. Join the blocks into horizontal rows. Then join rows to complete the quilt top as shown in the quilt assembly diagram on page 36. Press all seams open.

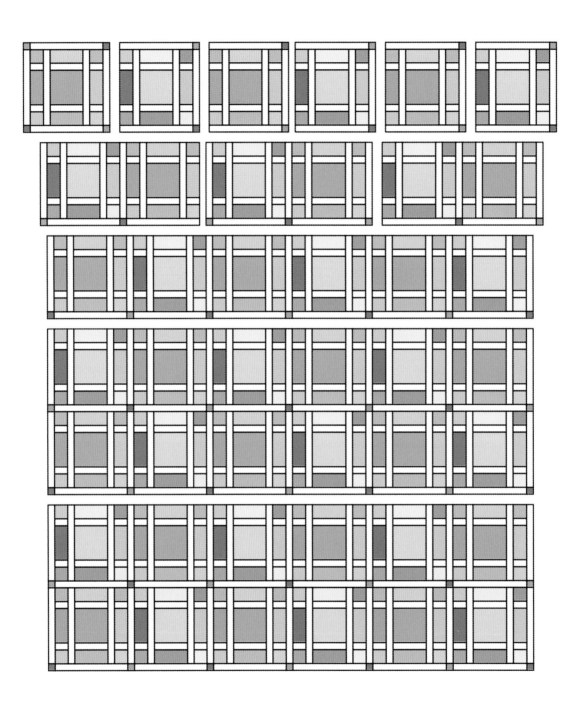

Quilt assembly diagram
(shown in Full size)

Crib   Twin   Full   King

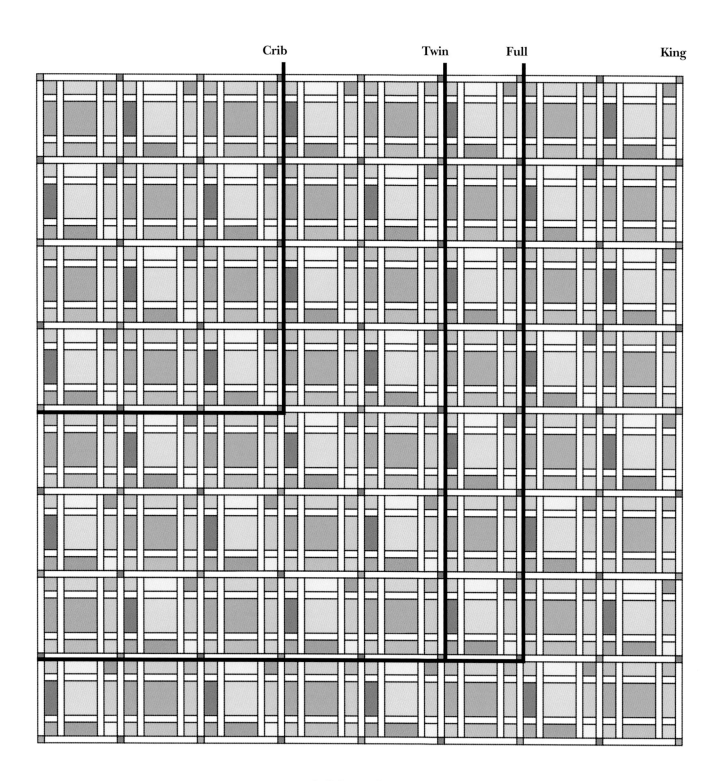

Quilt layout diagram

Bling

Quilted by Shelly Moore

When I saw Melody Miller's Social fabric collection for Ruby Star Society, and it was filled with a mix of fun, funky large prints and small supporting designs, I knew I wanted to come up with something that would allow me to use different-sized shapes to play up each design to its fullest. That's where the idea to use one large diamond surrounded by several small diamonds came from.

By adding a neutral sashing strip, I was able to coordinate the fabric in each diamond block and let them stand apart from each other. The result is a quilt that allows you to use big sections of that "too-pretty-to-cut-up" fabric surrounded by coordinates that make it look even more special. And the best part—this quilt is designed with no Y-seams!

Fabric Requirements

	Fat Quarters	Background	Binding	Backing	# of Blocks	Finished Size
Crib	5	1¼ yards (1.14m)	½ yard (0.46m)	1⅔ yards (1.53m)	18	35" x 46½" (0.89 x 1.18m)
Lap	13	2½ yards (2.29m)	¾ yard (0.69cm)	4 yards (3.66m)	46	61¼" x 62" (1.56 x 1.57m)
Twin	18	3½ yards (3.20m)	¾ yard (0.69cm)	5¾ yards (5.26m)	72	61¼" x 93" (1.56 x 2.36m)
Queen	30	4¾ yards (4.34m)	¾ yard (0.69cm)	8¾ yards (8.00m)	116	96¼" x 93" (2.44 x 2.36m)

Cutting Instructions

You must use a 60-degree triangle ruler with all three points, like the Clearview Triangle, in order to cut the right number of diamonds and triangles for this pattern. The cutting instructions will not work if you use a 60-degree triangle ruler with one blunt point.

FAT QUARTERS

1. Select two (six, eight, thirteen) fat quarters. Cut three 5" x 21" (12.70 x 53.34cm) strips from each.

2. Select a 5" (12.70cm) strip. Using a 60-degree triangle ruler, line the 5" (12.70cm) line up with the bottom of the strip and line up the point even with the top of the strip. Cut the corner off the strip, leaving a 60-degree angle on the edge of the strip.

Flip the 60-degree ruler over so that the 5" (12.70cm) line is even with the top of the strip and the point is even with the bottom of the strip. The left side of the ruler should be even with the top left point you just cut. Cut along the right side of the ruler to create a 60-degree diamond.

Continue sliding the ruler down to cut three 5" (12.70cm) diamonds from each strip, for a total of six 5" (12.70cm) diamonds from each fat quarter, for a total of eighteen (forty-six, seventy-two, 116) diamonds.

3. Select three (seven, ten, seventeen) fat quarters and cut six 2¾" x 21" (6.99 x 53.34cm) strips from each. Repeat Step 2 with the 2¾" x 21" (6.99 x 53.34cm) strips, cutting six 2¾" (6.99cm) diamonds from each strip, for a total of ninety (230, 360, 580) diamonds.

BACKGROUND

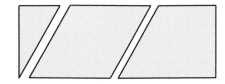

4. Cut one (two, three, three) 8¼" (20.96cm) x WOF strips. Unfold the fabric and cut diamonds according to Step 2 to create four diamonds per strip, for a total of four (six, ten, ten) diamonds.

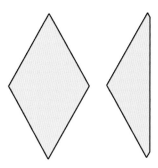

5. Align a ruler vertically with the ¼" (0.64cm) mark, even with the top and bottom points. Cut to make four (six, ten, ten) side setting triangles.

6. Cut one (two, two, three) 8½" (21.59cm) x WOF strips. Using a 60-degree triangle ruler, line the 5" (12.70cm) line up with the bottom of the strip and line up the point even with the top of the strip. Cut the corner off the strip, leaving a 60-degree angle on the edge of the strip. Square up the edge of the corner so that there is a ¼" (0.64cm) seam to the left of the center.

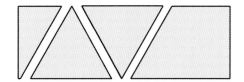

7. Cut down the right side of the ruler to create a 60-degree triangle. Flip the ruler so that the point is at the bottom of the strip and the left side of the ruler is even with the top left point of the strip that you just cut. Cut down the right side of the ruler.

Continue in this manner until you have cut seven setting triangles per strip, for a total of six (twelve, twelve, twenty) triangles and four corner setting triangles.

Cut nine (twenty-three, thirty-six, fifty-eight) 1½" (3.81cm) x WOF strips. Cross-cut into two 1½" x 9½" (3.81 x 24.13cm) rectangles and two 1½" x 10½" (3.81 x 26.67cm) rectangles, for a total of eighteen (forty-six, seventy-two, 116) 1½" x 9½" (3.81 x 24.13cm) rectangles and eighteen (forty-six, seventy-two, 116) 1½" x 10½" (3.81 x 26.67cm) rectangles.

BINDING

8. Cut five (seven, eight, ten) 2½" (6.35cm) x WOF strips.

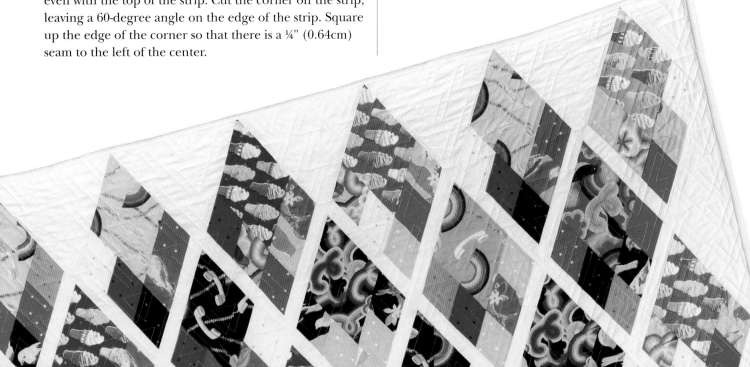

Block Assembly Instructions

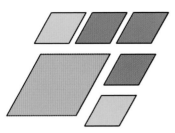

1. Select five 2¾" (6.99cm) diamonds and one 5" (12.70cm) diamond and arrange as shown above.

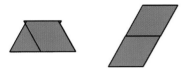

2. Place the small diamonds right sides together as shown above and sew a ¼" (0.64cm) seam. Press the seams open.

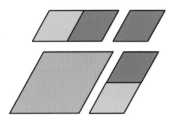

3. Join the top and bottom rows as shown above.

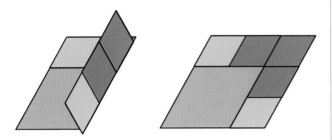

4. Sew the right row of small diamonds to the left row. Press the seams open.

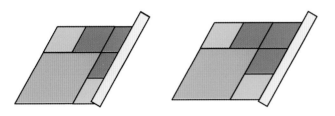

5. Select a 1½" x 9½" (3.81 x 24.13cm) rectangle. Arrange right sides together as shown above, with the rectangle ¼" (0.64cm) beyond the bottom right of the diamond block. Sew a ¼" (0.64cm) seam and press open.

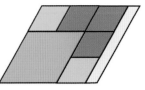

6. Trim the edges of the strip so that it is even with the edges of the diamond block.

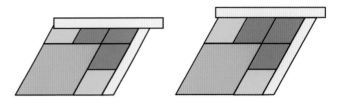

7. Repeat Steps 5 and 6 to sew the 1½" x 10½" (3.81 x 26.67cm) rectangle to the top of the block as shown above.

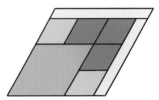

8. Trim the edges of the strip so that it is even with the edges of the diamond block. Repeat to make eighteen (forty-six, seventy-two, 116) blocks.

Quilt Assembly Instructions

1. Arrange the blocks and setting diamonds and triangles as shown in the quilt layout diagram on page 43.

2. Sew the blocks into diagonal rows as shown in the quilt assembly diagram on page 42. Then join the rows to complete the quilt top.

Quilt assembly diagram
(shown in Queen size)

Crib   **Lap/Twin**   **Queen**

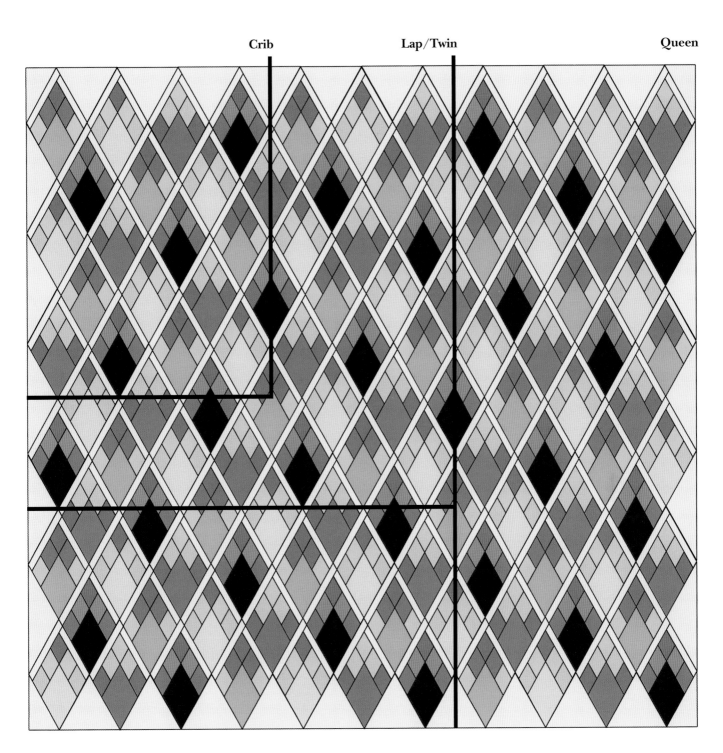

Quilt layout diagram

Cross & Dot

Sometimes you come across a fabric line that has a whole lot of neutral prints. That was the case with Summer Sampler by Nancy Nicholson for Clothworks. The fabrics in the bundle were evenly split into light, medium, and dark hues, which can make it challenging to use the entire fabric line and still be able to create contrast between the block and the background.

Because I loved the line and wanted to use all of it, I came up with a workaround that would use the lightest fabrics in the center of the block and the medium fabrics as rectangles surrounding the center square, then top it off with the darkest fabrics for the no-waste flying geese. And just like that, I was able to separate the very light neutral centers from the background to create clear, defined blocks.

Besides finding a way to use all the light prints in this collection, my favorite part of Cross & Dot is the secondary "dot" design created when the blocks are pieced together. It's such a fun way to see the fabrics come together.

Fabric Requirements

	Fat Quarters	Background	Backing	# of Blocks	Finished Size
Crib	1L, 3M, 1D	1½ yards (1.37m)	1¾ yards (1.60m)	12	36" x 48" (0.91 x 1.22m)
Lap	2L, 6M, 2D	2½ yards (2.29m)	3¼ yards (2.97m)	24	48" x 72" (1.22 x 1.83m)
Twin	4L, 12M, 4D	4½ yards (4.11m)	6 yards (5.49m)	48	72" x 96" (1.83 x 2.44m)
King	6L, 18M, 6D	6½ yards (5.94m)	9 yards (8.23m)	72	96" x 108" (2.44 x 2.74m)

L = light, M = medium, D = dark

Cutting Instructions

LIGHT FAT QUARTERS

1. From each light fat quarter, cut three 4½" x 21" (11.43 x 53.34cm) strips. Cross-cut each strip into four 4½" (11.43cm) squares, for a total of twelve (twenty-four, forty-eight, seventy-two) 4½" (11.43cm) squares.

MEDIUM FAT QUARTERS

2. From each medium fat quarter, cut seven 2½" x 21" (6.35 x 53.34cm) strips.

Cross-cut four strips into 2½" x 4½" (6.35 x 11.43cm) rectangles, for a total of forty-eight (ninety-six, 192, 288) rectangles.

Cross-cut two strips into 2½" (6.35cm) squares, for a total of forty-eight (ninety-six, 192, 288) squares.

Reserve the remaining strip for scrappy binding.

DARK FAT QUARTERS

3. From each dark fat quarter, cut three 5¼" x 21" (13.34 x 53.34cm) strips. Cross-cut into four 5¼" (13.34cm) squares, for a total of twelve (twenty-four, forty-eight, seventy-two) 5¼" (13.34cm) squares.

BACKGROUND

4. Cut six (twelve, twenty-four, thirty-six) 4½" (11.43cm) x WOF strips. Cross-cut the strips into 4½" (11.43cm) squares, for a total of forty-eight (ninety-six, 192, 288) 4½" (11.43cm) squares.

5. Cut four (seven, fourteen, twenty-one) 2⅞" (7.30cm) x WOF strips. Cross-cut the strips into 2⅞" (7.30cm) squares, for a total of forty-eight (ninety-six, 192, 288) 2⅞" (7.30cm) squares.

6. Cut four (three, three, two) 2½" (6.35cm) x WOF strips for scrappy binding.

Block Assembly Instructions

1. Select one background 4½" (11.43cm) square and one medium 2½" (6.35cm) square. Draw a line from corner to corner on the wrong side of the medium square.

2. Place the squares right sides together with the medium square in the upper right corner as shown above. Sew on the drawn line.

3. Place the ¼" (0.64cm) line of your ruler on the drawn line and trim off the corner, leaving a ¼" (0.64cm) seam extending past the drawn line. Press the seam open.

4. Repeat Steps 1–3 to create forty-eight (ninety-six, 192, 288). If you want to have all four corners of the block match, create twelve (twenty-four, forty-eight, seventy-two) matched sets of four.

5. Select one dark 5¼" (13.34cm) square and two background 2⅞" (7.30cm) squares. Draw a line from corner to corner on the wrong side of the background squares.

6. Arrange the background squares as shown above with right sides together. Sew a scant ¼" (0.64cm) seam down both sides of the drawn lines.

7. Cut the squares apart on the drawn line. Press seams open so that the background triangles are facing away from the dark triangle.

8. Select two more 2⅞" (7.30cm) background squares. Draw a line from corner to corner on the wrong side of the background squares and arrange them right sides together, as shown above, with the dark triangle. Sew a scant ¼" (0.64cm) seam down both sides of the drawn line.

9. Cut the units apart on the drawn line. Press the seams open to reveal four flying geese. Trim to 2½" x 4½" (6.35 x 11.43cm).

10. Repeat Steps 5–9 to create forty-eight (ninety-six, 192, 288) flying geese. You will already have matched sets of four by making four-at-a-time no-waste flying geese.

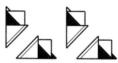

11. Select a flying geese from Step 9 and a medium 2½"x 4½" (6.35 x 11.43cm) rectangle. Sew together and press the seams open. Repeat to create forty-eight (ninety-six, 192, 288). If you want to have all four crosses of the block match, create twelve (twenty-four, forty-eight, seventy-two) matched sets of four.

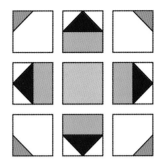

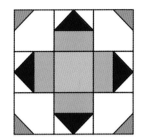

12. Select four units from Step 3, four units from Step 11, and one light 4½" (11.43cm) square. Arrange as shown above. If you want the corners and crosses to match, make sure to select the matched sets of four as you lay out your block.

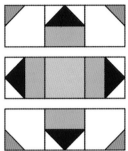

13. Sew the block into horizontal rows. Press the seams open.

14. Join the rows to complete the block. Press the seams open. Make a total of twelve (twenty-four, forty-eight, seventy-two) blocks.

Quilt Assembly Instructions

1. Arrange the blocks into a design that is pleasing to you according to the quilt layout diagram on page 49.

2. Join the blocks into horizontal rows. Then join the rows to complete the quilt top as shown in the quilt assembly diagram on page 48. Press all seams open.

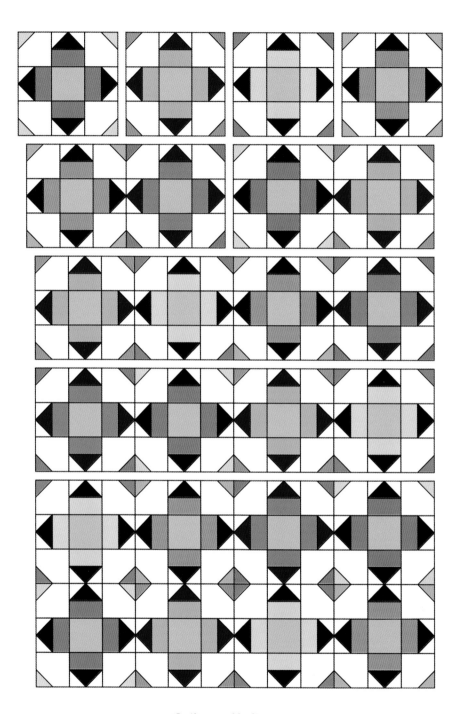

Quilt assembly diagram
(shown in Lap size)

Crib   Lap   Twin   King

Quilt layout diagram

En Pointe

E n Pointe was designed one month into a statewide lockdown during the beginning of the COVID-19 pandemic. I went from working a little here and there while on maternity leave to trying to fill orders from my living room all day and night, while at the same time my kindergartener did remote learning at the table next to me, my husband shipped packages from our hallway, and the baby slept in a bouncy seat at my feet. We also were cooking every meal, which included baking sandwich bread, starting seeds, and pulling up sod for a vegetable garden. To say it was a crazy time is an understatement.

When I also had to add designing and making a quilt for our Stashin' with Stephanie subscription club to my to-do list, I knew I wanted something that was super easy but didn't look like it. The block technique for En Pointe comes from my good friend Char Thode's book *Nickel Quilts*. We transform two large squares into two half-square triangles and two smaller squares very easily and quickly.

The quilt is assembled in horizontal rows, but the modern setting creates the appearance of a quilt that is designed on point. The visual effect is fun and makes En Pointe look a lot more complicated than it really is. My daughter was doing her weekly ballet lessons on Zoom while I was designing the quilt, which inspired the name.

Fabric Requirements

	Fat Quarters	Background	Binding	Backing	# of blocks	Finished Size
Crib	4	1¼ yards (1.14m)	½ yard (0.46m)	1½ yards (1.37m)	30	35" x 42" (0.89 x 1.07m)
Lap	11	2¾ yards (2.51m)	⅔ yard (0.61m)	4¼ yards (3.89m)	81	63" x 63" (1.60x 1.60m)
Twin	15	3¾ yards (3.43m)	¾ yard (0.69m)	5⅔ yards (5.18m)	117	63" x 91" (1.60 x 2.31m)
King	29	7 yards (6.40m)	1 yard (0.91m)	9¾ yards (8.92m)	225	105" x 105" (2.67 x 2.67m)

Cutting Instructions

FAT QUARTERS

1. From each fat quarter, cut two 8½" x 21" (21.59 x 53.34cm) strips. Cross-cut each strip into two 8½" (21.59cm) squares, for a total of fifteen (forty-one, fifty-nine, 113) 8½-inch (21.59cm) squares.

BACKGROUND

2. Cut four (eleven, fifteen, twenty-nine) 8½" (21.59cm) x WOF strips. Cross-cut each strip into four 8½" (21.59cm) squares, for a total of fifteen (forty-one, fifty-nine, 113) 8½" (21.59cm) squares.

BINDING

3. Cut five (seven, eight, eleven) 2½" (6.35cm) x WOF strips.

Block Assembly Instructions

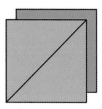

1. Select fifteen (forty-one, fifty-nine, 113) 8½" (21.59cm) squares from the fat quarters and fifteen (forty-one, fifty-nine, 113) 8½" (21.59cm) squares from the background fabric. Draw a line from corner to corner on the wrong side of the background squares and arrange right sides together with the fat quarter squares.

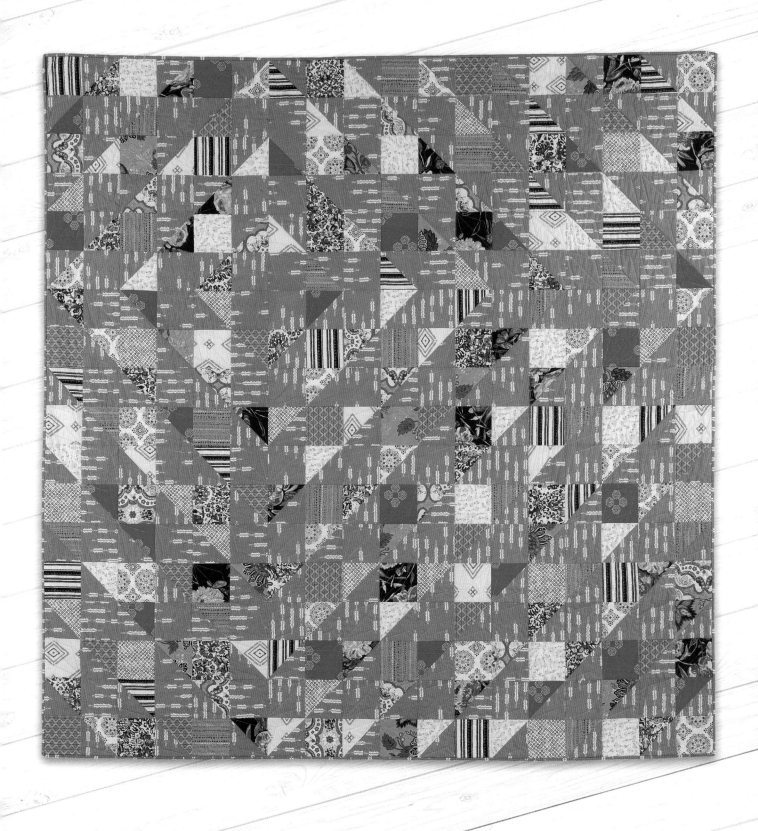

2. Sew a scant ¼" (0.64cm) seam down both sides of the drawn line.

3. Cut apart along the drawn line to reveal two half-square triangles per square unit. You will need a total of thirty (eighty-one, 117, 225) half-square triangles. Press seams open and trim to 8" (20.32cm) square.

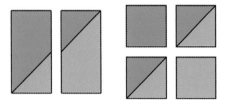

4. Place the 4" (10.16cm) mark of your ruler along the vertical edge of the block and cut in half. Without moving the block, lift the ruler and place the 4" (10.16cm) mark on the bottom of the block and cut in half horizontally.

You should now have two 4" (10.16cm) half-square triangles and two 4" (10.16cm) squares per 8" (20.32cm) half-square triangle, for a total of sixty (162, 234, 450) 4" (10.16cm) half-square triangles and sixty (162, 234, 450) 4" (10.16cm) squares.

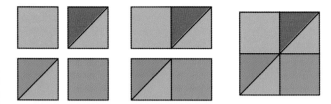

5. Arrange half-square triangles and squares from Step 4 as shown above in the left-hand diagram. Sew together into two horizontal rows, then into one block. Press all seams open. The block should measure 7½" (19.05cm) square. Repeat to make thirty (eighty-one, 117, 225) blocks.

Quilt Assembly Instructions

1. Arrange the blocks into a quilt design that is pleasing to you. Pay attention to the direction in which the half-square triangles are pointing to create the focal point in the top left corner. See the quilt layout diagram on the facing page.

2. Sew the blocks into horizontal rows as shown below in the quilt assembly diagram. Then join the rows to complete the quilt top, pressing all seams open. This is illustrated in the quilt assembly diagram below, which shows the lap-sized version of the quilt.

Quilt assembly diagram
(shown in Lap size)

Crib Lap/Twin King

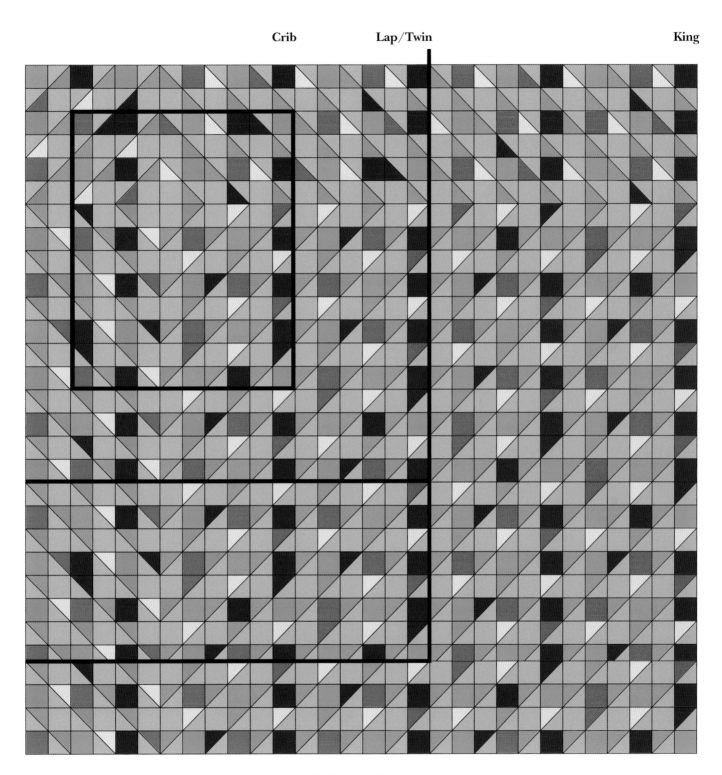

Quilt layout diagram

Geometric Garden

Quilted by Shelly Moore

I am a big fan of the bright colors you often find in FIGO Fabrics collections, but Flora by Marisol Ortega is extra fun, with bold, vibrant colors and modern florals that really pop against a neutral backdrop. One night, when sleep eluded me, I had this vision of a pinwheel-like block that looked like a geometric flower in an alternating setting to make it look like an actual garden plot where the flowers are spaced out just so.

It took some figuring, but there are two kinds of blocks for this quilt: a full block and a skinny block that is completed when you put it next to a full block. And the best part of this quilt? There are no triangle points to match anywhere in the entire quilt! So you can have all the beauty of half-square triangles without the headache of getting the points to line up right.

Fabric Requirements

	Fat Quarters	Background	Binding	Backing	Finished Size
Crib	4	1¼ yards (1.14m)	½ yard (0.46m)	1½ yards (1.37m)	39" x 45" (0.99 x 1.14m)
Lap	11	3 yards (2.74m)	⅔ yard (0.61m)	4¾ yards (4.34m)	63" x 75" (1.6 x 1.91m)
Twin	13	3½ yards (3.20m)	¾ yard (0.69m)	5⅔ yards (5.18m)	63" x 90" (1.6 x 2.29m)
King	27	7 yards (6.40m)	1 yard (0.91m)	9¾ yards (8.92m)	111" x 105" (2.82 x 2.67m)

Cutting Instructions

FAT QUARTERS

1. From each fat quarter, cut two 3½" x 21" (8.89 x 53.34cm) strips and two 4" x 21" (10.16 x 53.34cm) strips.

2. Cross-cut each 3½" (8.89cm) strip into six 3½" (8.89cm) squares, for a total of forty-eight (132, 156, 324) 3½" (8.89cm) squares.

3. Cross cut each 4" (10.16cm) strip into five 4" (10.16cm) squares, for a total of forty (110, 130, 270) 4" (10.16cm) squares.

BACKGROUND

4. Cut six (sixteen, nineteen, thirty-nine) 3½" (8.89cm) x WOF strips. Cross-cut each 3½" (8.89cm) strip into twelve 3½" (8.89cm) squares, for a total of seventy-two (190, 228, 462) 3½" (8.89cm) background squares.

5. Cut four (eleven, thirteen, twenty-seven) 4" (10.16cm) x WOF strips. Cross-cut each 4" (10.16cm) strip into twelve 4" (10.16cm) squares, for a total of forty (110, 130, 270) 4" (10.16cm) background squares.

BINDING

6. Cut five (seven, eight, eleven) 2½" (6.35cm) x WOF strips.

Block Assembly Instructions

1. Select thirty-nine (105, 126, 259) 4" (10.16cm) squares from the fat quarters and thirty-nine (105, 126, 259) 4" (10.16cm) squares from the background fabric. Draw a line from corner to corner on the wrong side of the background squares and arrange right sides together with the fat quarter squares.

2. Sew a scant ¼" (0.64cm) seam down both sides of the drawn line.

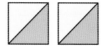

3. Cut apart along the drawn line to reveal two half-square triangles per square unit. You will have a total of seventy-eight (210, 252, 518) squares. Press the seams open and trim to 3½" (8.89cm) square.

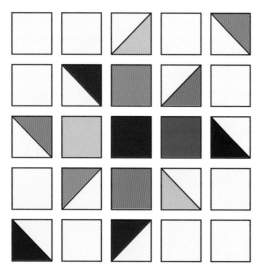

4. Arrange half-square triangles with five 3½" (8.89cm) squares from fat quarters in the block center inside the star points, and ten 3½" (8.89cm) background squares in the block corners outside of the star per block.

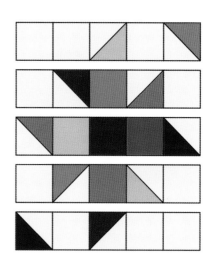

5. Sew into horizontal rows, pressing the seams open.

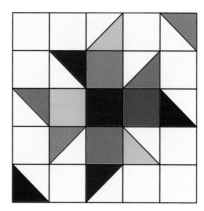

6. Sew the rows together to complete the block, pressing the seams open. Create a total of five (thirteen, sixteen, twenty-nine) blocks. Blocks should measure 15½" (39.37cm) square.

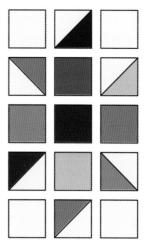

7. Arrange half-square triangles with five 3½" (8.89cm) squares from fat quarters in the block center inside the star points, and four 3½" (8.89cm) background squares in the block corners outside of the star.

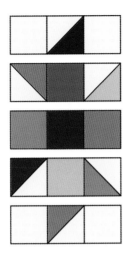

8. Sew into horizontal rows, pressing the seams open.

9. Sew the rows together to complete the block, pressing the seams open. Create a total of two (eight, ten, twenty-five) blocks. Blocks should measure 9½" x 15½" (24.13 x 39.37cm).

10. This quilt is assembled in staggered rows to create the interlocking flower design. To accomplish this, many of the blocks at the top and bottom of the row are assembled in part, so that the bottom of the block is sewn to the top of the row and the top of the block sewn to the bottom.

Refer to the partial block assembly diagram below to determine which configurations you need to make for your size quilt. Assemble the partial blocks into horizontal rows, then join the rows just like as in the other blocks, pressing the seams open.

Quilt Assembly Instructions

1. Arrange the blocks into a quilt design that is pleasing to you, paying attention to the location of the partial blocks to create the staggered rows. See the quilt layout diagram on page 59, which includes all quilt sizes.

Be sure to alternate rows of 15½" (39.37cm) square blocks with rows of 9½" x 15½" (24.13 x 39.37cm) blocks as shown in the quilt assembly diagram on page 58. All sizes begin and end with a row of 15½" (39.37cm) square blocks.

2. Sew the blocks into vertical rows as shown in the quilt assembly diagram, then join the rows to complete the quilt top, pressing all the seams open. This is illustrated in the quilt assembly diagram, which shows the lap-sized version of the quilt.

Partial Block Assembly Diagram

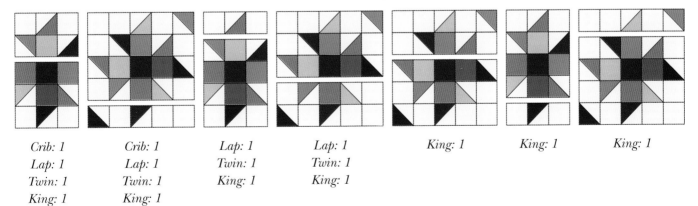

Crib: 1
Lap: 1
Twin: 1
King: 1

Crib: 1
Lap: 1
Twin: 1
King: 1

Lap: 1
Twin: 1
King: 1

Lap: 1
Twin: 1
King: 1

King: 1

King: 1

King: 1

Quilt assembly diagram
(shown in Lap size)

Crib **Lap/Twin** **King**

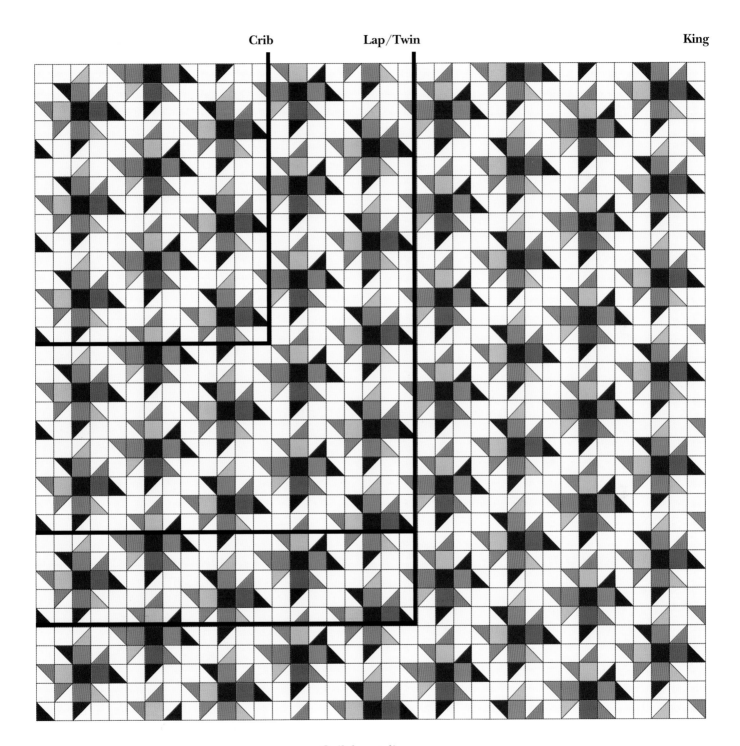

Quilt layout diagram

Lily Field

When I was making this quilt, there was an intense debate going on in my house over what our second daughter should be named. My five-year-old and I wanted Lily. My husband wasn't sure what he wanted, but Lily wasn't it. I was eight months pregnant, and it was looking like I wasn't going to get the name I wanted, so I named this quilt Lily Field instead. I thought the six-pointed stars looked a lot like stargazer lilies, and I'd at least get to name something Lily.

This quilt is made by first strip piecing and then cutting the strips into equilateral triangles. Then you lay everything out how you want it and sew it back together in horizontal rows to avoid any pesky Y-seams. The result is a simple construction that looks much harder than it is. And I love how Meriweather from Art Gallery Fabrics creates a fun alternation of color from the pink and green diamonds.

And after much discussion, the girls prevailed, and we welcomed future quilter Lily Jean Soebbing into the world. This quilt will be hers someday.

Fabric Requirements

	Fat Quarters	Background	Binding	Backing	Finished Size
Crib	7	1¼ yards (1.14m)	½ yard (0.46m)	2 yards (1.83m)	39¾" x 57½" (1.01 x 1.46m)
Lap	14	2¼ yards (2.06m)	⅔ yard (0.61m)	4¾ yards (4.34m)	59⅝" x 74¾" (1.52 x 1.90m)
Twin	18	2½ yards (2.29m)	¾ yard (0.69m)	5⅔ yards (5.18m)	59⅝" x 92" (1.51 x 2.34m)
King	35	5 yards (4.57m)	1 yard (0.91m)	9¼ yards (8.46m)	99⅜" x 109¼" (2.52 x 2.77m)

Cutting Instructions

FAT QUARTERS

1. From each fat quarter, cut five 3½" x 21" (8.89 x 53.34cm) strips, for a total of thirty-four (sixty-eight, eighty-six, 174) strips.

BACKGROUND

2. Cut six (eleven, thirteen, twenty-six) 6½" (16.51cm) x WOF strips.

BINDING

3. Cut six (seven, eight, eleven) 2½" (6.35cm) x WOF strips.

Block Assembly Instructions

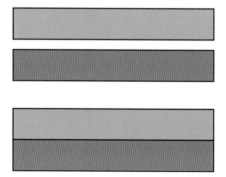

1. Select two 3½" x 21" (8.89 x 53.34cm) strips from the fat quarters. We paired light strips and dark strips together. Sew the strips together along the long side using a ¼" (0.64cm) seam. Press seam open.

Repeat with the remaining 3½" x 21" (8.89 x 53.34cm) strips to create seventeen (thirty-four, forty-three, eighty-seven) strip sets.

Note: For the next section, you must use a 60-degree triangle ruler with all three points, like the Clearview Triangle, in order to cut the right number of diamonds and triangles for this pattern. The cutting instructions will not work if you use a 60-degree triangle ruler with one blunt point.

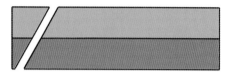

2. Using a 60-degree triangle ruler, line the 6½" (16.51cm) line up with the bottom of the strip set and line up the point even with the top of the strip set. Cut the corner off the strip set, leaving a 60-degree angle on the edge of the strip set. Trim the corner of the half-equilateral triangle so that you have a ¼" (0.64cm) seam extending beyond the triangle point.

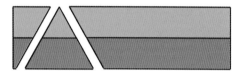

3. Leaving the ruler in place, cut along the right side of the ruler to create a 60-degree triangle.

4. Flip the 60-degree ruler over so that the 6½" (16.51cm) line is even with the top of the strip set and the point is even with the bottom of the strip set. The left side of the ruler should be even with the top left point you just cut. Cut along the right side of the ruler to create a 60-degree triangle.

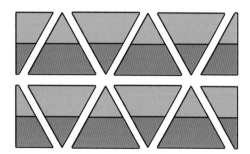

5. Repeat Steps 2–4 to cut four triangles from each strip set. To ensure you have enough half-equilateral triangles to create half-diamonds on the sides of the quilt, alternate the orientation of the ruler on every other strip set as shown above.

You need a total of sixty-eight (136, 172, 348) equilateral triangles and eight (sixteen, sixteen, twenty-four) half-equilateral triangles.

6. With the background strip folded in half, cut eight equilateral triangles and two half-equilateral triangles from each of the 6½" (16.51cm) x WOF strips. You will get eight equilateral triangles from each strip, for a total of forty-two (eighty-five, 100, 203) equilateral triangles and twelve (ten, sixteen, fourteen) half-equilateral triangles.

Quilt Assembly Instructions

This quilt is assembled in horizontal rows to avoid sewing Y-seams. If you are unable to lay out the entire quilt and leave it out until the entire top is finished, try laying out two to four rows at a time each time you have a chance to sew.

1. Arrange equilateral and half-equilateral triangles as shown in the quilt layout diagram on page 65. For the bottom row, replace the pieced triangle of the top star with a background triangle as shown on the quilt assembly diagram on page 64.

2. Working one row at a time, sew the triangles and half-equilateral triangles into sets of two matching seams when needed. Then join the sets of two into sets of four, then the sets of four into sets of eight, and so on until the row is joined. Press all seams open. This process is illustrated in the quilt assembly diagram.

3. Once your rows are assembled, join them into sets of two, then sets of four, and so on until the top is completed. Press all seams open.

4. Sew a ⅛" (0.32cm) seam around the entire quilt top to stabilize the bias edges before quilting.

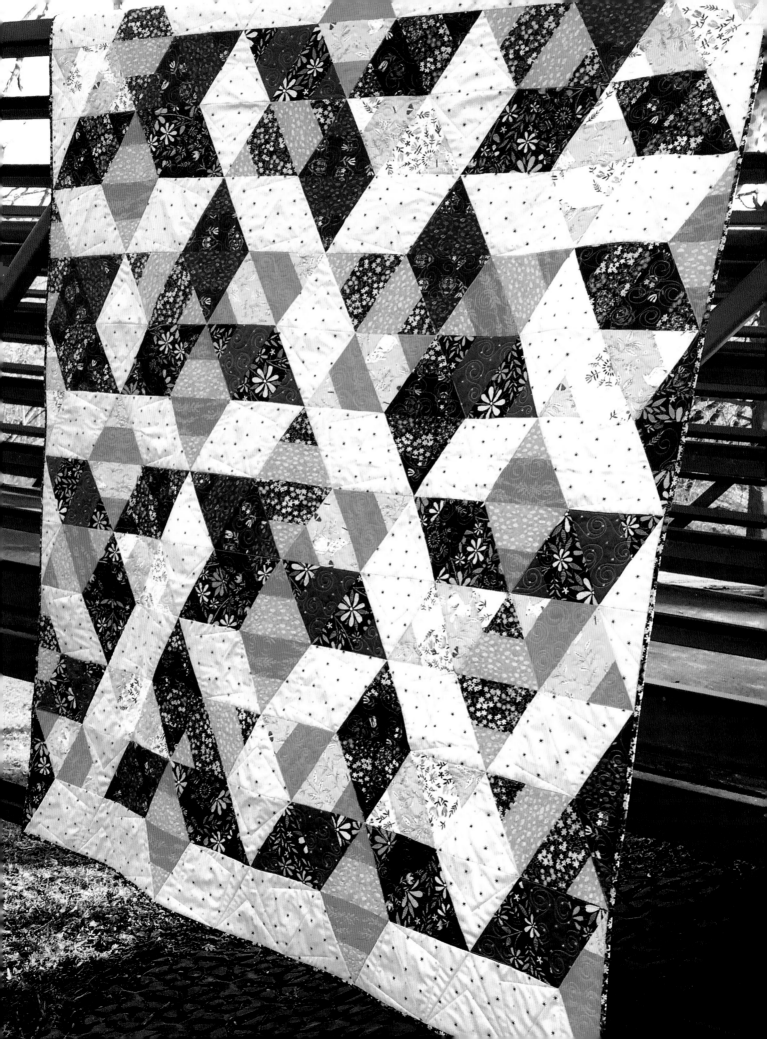

Quilt assembly diagram
(shown in Lap size)

Quilt layout diagram

Rainbow Frosting

I love a good no-neutral rainbow quilt. One of my first and most popular quilt designs used a matching 10" (25.40cm) charm pack and 2½" (6.35cm) strip roll to create a similar effect to Rainbow Frosting. I loved it, and still do, but finding matching 10" (25.40cm) charm packs and 2½" (6.35cm) strip rolls can sometimes be a daunting task. For Rainbow Frosting, I resized the diamonds and "fat quarter-fied" the pattern so it could be made with any of your favorite rainbow fat quarter bundles.

I used Kismet by Valori Wells for FreeSpirit and split the collection into six color groupings of three similar colors each. Each color grouping makes up one section of diamonds and fades into the next to create fun peaks that transform from one color to the next with no background fabric required. For the quilting, because there is so much going on with the quilt top, I just quilted it in horizontal straight lines, changing the top thread color to match the dominant color in the diamonds for that row of the quilt. It adds subtle texture without taking away from the diamond peaks or the color change of the fabric.

Fabric Requirements

	Fat Quarters	Binding	Backing	Finished Size
Lap	18*	½ yard (0.46m)	3½ yards (3.2m)	52½" x 58½" (1.33 x 1.49m)

* To create the color changes in the diamond peaks, split your fat quarters into six groups of three similar colors. When creating your pieced diamonds, use three colors to make each set of strip-pieced and whole diamonds.

Cutting Instructions

You must use a 60-degree triangle ruler with all three points, like the Clearview Triangle, in order to cut the right number of diamonds and triangles for this pattern. The cutting instructions will not work if you use a 60-degree triangle ruler with one blunt point.

FAT QUARTERS

1. From each fat quarter, cut two 4" x 21" (10.16 x 53.34cm) strips and four 2¼" x 21" (5.72 x 53.34cm) strips.

BINDING

2. Cut six 2½" (6.35cm) x WOF strips.

Assembly Instructions

1. Select a 4" (10.16cm) strip. With the 4" (10.16cm) mark on the equilateral triangle ruler even with the top of the strip, and the point ¼" (0.64cm) away from the bottom left of the strip, cut a 4" (10.16cm)–tall half-equilateral triangle. You will have a ¼" (0.64cm) seam allowance to the left of the triangle center.

2. Turn the equilateral triangle ruler so the 4" (10.16cm) mark is even with the bottom of the strip, the left side is even with the cut edge, and the point is even with the top of the strip. Cut along the right side of the ruler to create a 4" (10.16cm)–tall equilateral triangle.

3. Continue turning the ruler until you have cut seven equilateral triangles and two half-equilateral triangles from each strip, for a total of 252 equilateral triangles and seventy-two half-equilateral triangles.

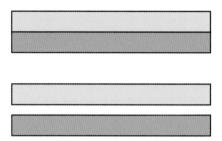

4. Select twelve 2¼" x 21" (5.72 x 53.34cm) strips from one colorway. Sew the strips together along the long seam into sets of two, using a ¼" seam and making sure to mix up the pairing of fabrics. You will have six strip sets per colorway. Press the seams open.

Repeat with the remaining five colorways to create a total of thirty-six strip sets.

5. Using the techniques from Steps 1–3, cut seven equilateral triangles from each strip set, for a total of 252 equilateral triangles.

The strip-pieced half-equilateral triangles are not used in this project. Save them for a bonus throw pillow or a pieced back.

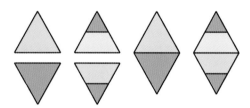

6. Arrange the equilateral triangles from Steps 3 and 5 together. Sew them together into a whole and strip-pieced diamond, keeping like colors together. Press the seams open.

Note: Set thirteen equilateral triangles aside from the two colorways that will make up the top and bottom rows. *Do not* sew them together. They will remain as triangles in the final construction.

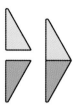

7. Sew the half-equilateral triangles together to form half-diamonds. You will need up to four from each colorway. Leave two half-equilateral triangles from the first and last colorways unsewn to make up the corners in the final construction.

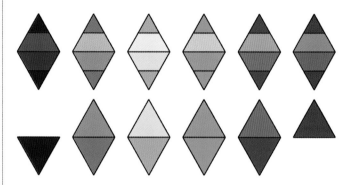

8. When you are ready to assemble the quilt, you should have:
- Twenty-one of each colorway of the strip-pieced diamonds
- Twenty of the middle four colorways of the whole diamonds
- Thirteen of the first and last colorways of equilateral triangles
- Four of the first and last colorways of the half-equilateral triangles
- Four of the middle four colorways of the half-diamonds

Note: You will have some leftover whole diamonds and half diamonds.

9. Arrange the diamonds, triangles, half-triangles, and half-diamonds according to the quilt layout diagram on page 70.

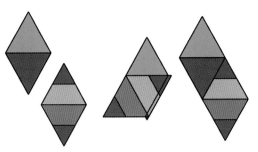

11. Sew the rows together to complete the quilt top.

12. Sew a ⅛" (0.32cm) seam around the edges of the quilt top to stabilize the edges for quilting and to keep the bias edges from stretching.

10. Sew diamonds together along the diagonal seam as shown in the quilt assembly diagram on page 71. When you place the diamonds right sides together, they will point in opposite directions until the seams are pressed open. Make sure to match your diamond points with the seam dog ears for accurate piecing.

Quilt design

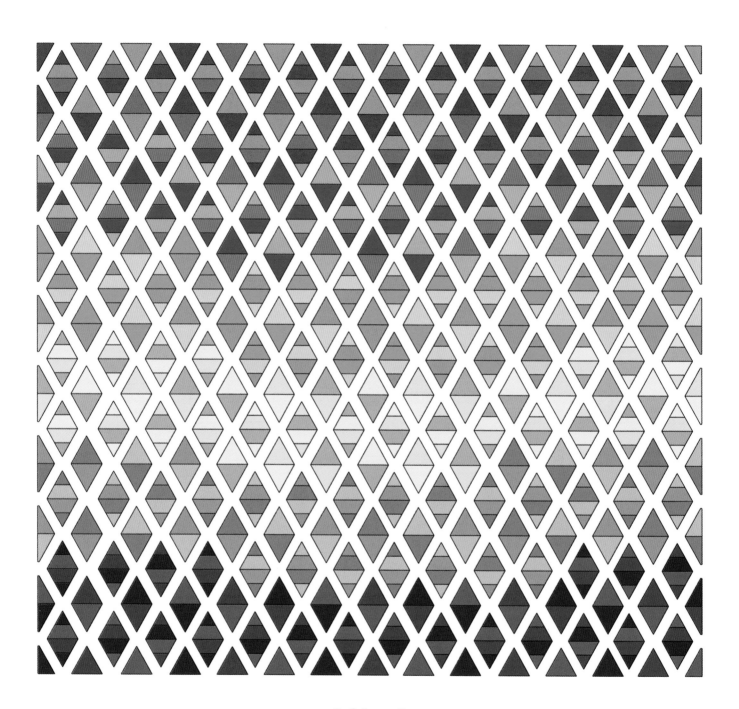

Quilt layout diagram

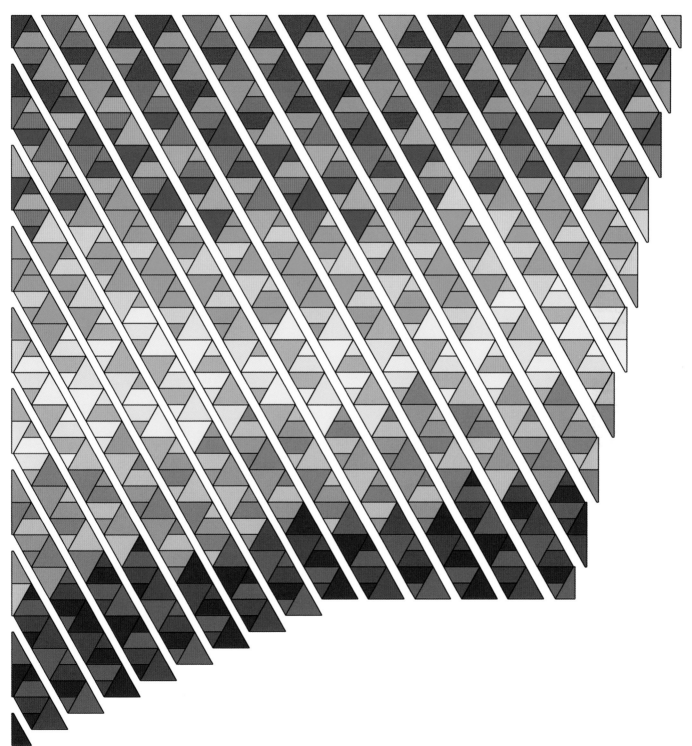

Quilt assembly diagram

Ray of Sunshine

I am a big fan of Pippa Shaw, but her collection Mountain Meadow for FIGO Fabrics was not my first choice for Stashin' with Stephanie. As states started to shut down one-by-one in March of 2020 due to COVID-19, we had to move fast to get our next two months' worth of subscription-club fabric in house just in case our fabric companies weren't allowed into their warehouses to ship. Typically, I choose collections to feature six months in advance, but we worked with FIGO to create a curated bundle of Mountain Meadow and Lucky Charms Basics that formed a beautifully coordinated rainbow, and we got it shipped the same day to try to beat the lockdown.

The result is a no-neutral quilt of carefully planned half-square triangle combinations that create the rainbow you see in the final quilt. It is also a perfect example of how a great stash of basics can help elevate and accentuate a fabulous collection when you don't quite have enough fat quarters in a bundle to complete a quilt you have fallen in love with.

Fabric Requirements

	Fat Quarters	Backing	Finished size
Lap	24	4¾ yards (4.34m)	64" x 72" (1.63 x 1.83m)

Cutting Instructions

FAT QUARTERS

From each fat quarter, cut three 5" x 21" (12.70 x 53.34cm) strips and one 2½" x 21" (6.35 x 53.34cm) strip. Cross-cut each 5" (12.70cm) strip into four 5" (12.70cm) squares, for a total of twelve 5" (12.70cm) squares per fat quarter and 288 5" (12.70cm) squares total.

Set the 2½" (6.35cm) strips aside for scrappy binding.

Block Assembly Instructions

1. Label the fabrics in color order from 1 to 24 (see page 74). Select six 5" (12.70cm) squares each from Fabrics 1 and 2. Draw a line from corner to corner on the wrong side of the Fabric 2 squares and arrange right sides together with the Fabric 1 squares.

2. Sew a scant ¼" (0.64cm) seam down both sides of the drawn line.

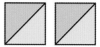

3. Cut apart along the drawn line to reveal two half-square triangles per square unit. Create a total of twelve half-square triangles from Fabrics 1 and 2.
Press the seams open and trim to 4½" (11.43cm) square.

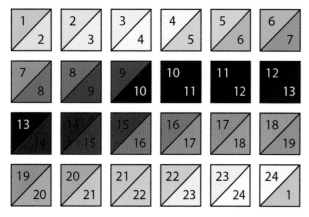

Quilt Assembly Instructions

1. Arrange the blocks according to the quilt layout diagram below.

2. Sew the blocks into horizontal rows, first joining the blocks into sets of two, then sets of four, then sets of eight, and then completing the row. Join the rows to complete the quilt top, pressing all seams open as shown in the quilt assembly diagram on the facing page.

4. Repeat Steps 1–3 to create twelve half-square triangles from each of the following 5" (12.70cm) square/half-square triangle combinations:
- Six of Fabric 2 and six of Fabric 3
- Six of Fabric 3 and six of Fabric 4
- Six of Fabric 4 and six of Fabric 5
- Six of Fabric 5 and six of Fabric 6
- Six of Fabric 6 and six of Fabric 7
- Six of Fabric 7 and six of Fabric 8
- Six of Fabric 8 and six of Fabric 9
- Six of Fabric 9 and six of Fabric 10
- Six of Fabric 10 and six of Fabric 11
- Six of Fabric 11 and six of Fabric 12
- Six of Fabric 12 and six of Fabric 13
- Six of Fabric 13 and six of Fabric 14
- Six of Fabric 14 and six of Fabric 15
- Six of Fabric 15 and six of Fabric 16
- Six of Fabric 16 and six of Fabric 17
- Six of Fabric 17 and six of Fabric 18
- Six of Fabric 18 and six of Fabric 19
- Six of Fabric 19 and six of Fabric 20
- Six of Fabric 20 and six of Fabric 21
- Six of Fabric 21 and six of Fabric 22
- Six of Fabric 22 and six of Fabric 23
- Six of Fabric 23 and six of Fabric 24
- Six of Fabric 24 and six of Fabric 1

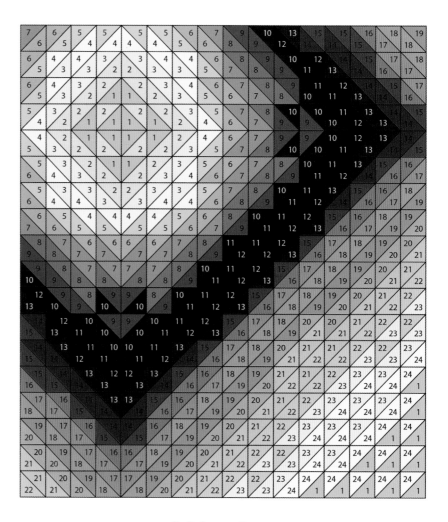

Quilt layout diagram

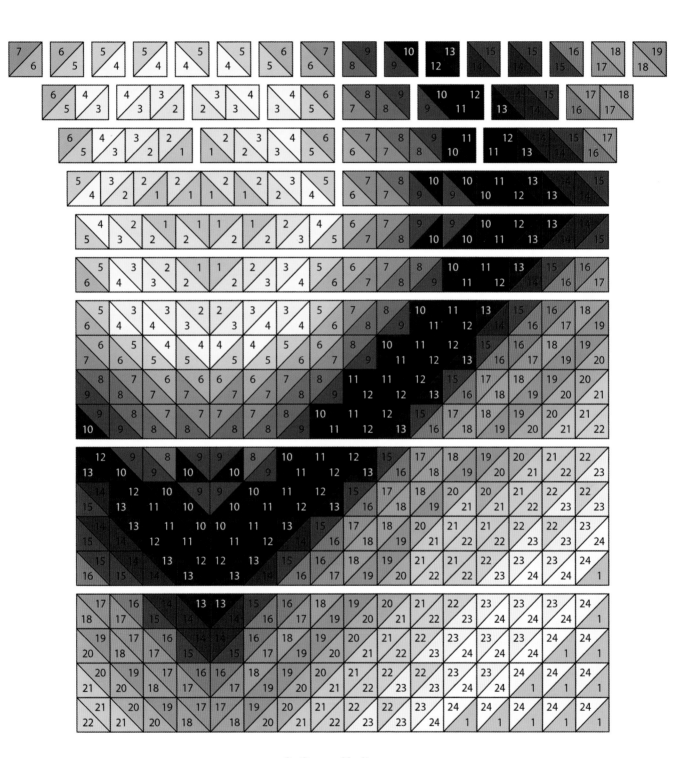

Quilt assembly diagram

Strata

After more than three years of working alongside me every day in our business, my husband now has opinions about fabric. And he was not so sure about Warehouse District by Wishwell for Robert Kaufman Fabrics. The digitally printed fabric pushes the boundaries of fabric design. With its layers reminiscent of peeling paint and downtown graffiti, it was pretty far from the fabrics I typically work with. But I told him to just wait and see what I did with it.

The design looked not only like graffiti; I thought it also looked like the layers of sediment that form rock walls when a road is cut straight into the side of a hill. I devised a quilt design that alternated strip-pieced small squares with long strips to let the fabric shine while also creating those rock-like layers that show off the colors together.

The result was an instant best-seller, as we sold out of the kit twice. The original fabrics might be hard to come by, but this is a great pattern for fabrics that are too pretty to cut up or those new digital prints that you just want to use big.

Fabric Requirements

	Fat Quarters	Background	Backing	Finished Size
Crib	6	1½ yards (1.37m)	2 yards (1.83m)	37" x 61" (0.94 x 1.55m)
Lap	9	2¼ yards (2.06m)	4 yards (3.66m)	61" x 61" (1.55 x 1.55m)
Full	14	3 yards (2.74m)	5 yards (4.57m)	73" x 81" (1.85 x 2.06m)
King	24	5¼ yards (4.80m)	9¼ yards (8.46m)	101" x 101" (2.57 x 2.57m)

Cutting Instructions

FAT QUARTERS

1. From each fat quarter, cut five 3½" x 21" (8.89 x 53.34cm) strips, for a total of twenty-eight (forty-two, sixty-six, 117) strips.

BACKGROUND

2. Cut twenty-six (thirty-eight, fifty-eight, 102) 1½" (3.81cm) x WOF strips.

3. Select eight (ten, fifteen, twenty-eight) strips and cut in half at the fold to create fifteen (twenty, thirty, fifty-five) 1½" x 21" (3.81cm x 53.34cm) strips.

4. Select two (two, three, six) strips and cross-cut into 1½" x 3½" (3.81 x 8.89cm) rectangles, for a total of thirteen (twenty-two, thirty-six, sixty-two) rectangles.

5. Select fifteen (twenty-four, thirty-eight, sixty-five) strips and cross-cut into the following lengths for the vertical sashing:
   - Crib: Ten 1½" x 40½" (3.81 x 102.87cm) strips and ten 1½" x 20½" (3.81 x 52.07cm) strips
   - Throw: Sixteen 1½" x 40½" (3.81 x 102.87cm) strips and sixteen 1½" x 20½" (3.81 x 52.07cm) strips
   - Full: Thirty-eight 1½" x 40½" (3.81 x 102.87cm) strips
   - King: Fifty-two 1½" x 40½" (3.81 x 102.87cm) strips and twenty-six 1½" x 20½" (3.81 x 52.07cm) strips

6. Select one (two, two, three) strips and cross-cut into the following lengths for the top sashing:
   - Crib: One 1½" x 37½" (3.81 x 95.25cm) strip
   - Throw: Two 1½" x 30½" (3.81 x 77.47cm) strips
   - Full: Two 1½" x 36½" (3.81 x 92.71cm) strips
   - King: Two 1½" x 40½" (3.81 x 102.87cm) strips and one 21½" (54.61cm) strip

7. Cut five (seven, eight, eleven) 2½" (6.35cm) x WOF strips for scrappy binding.

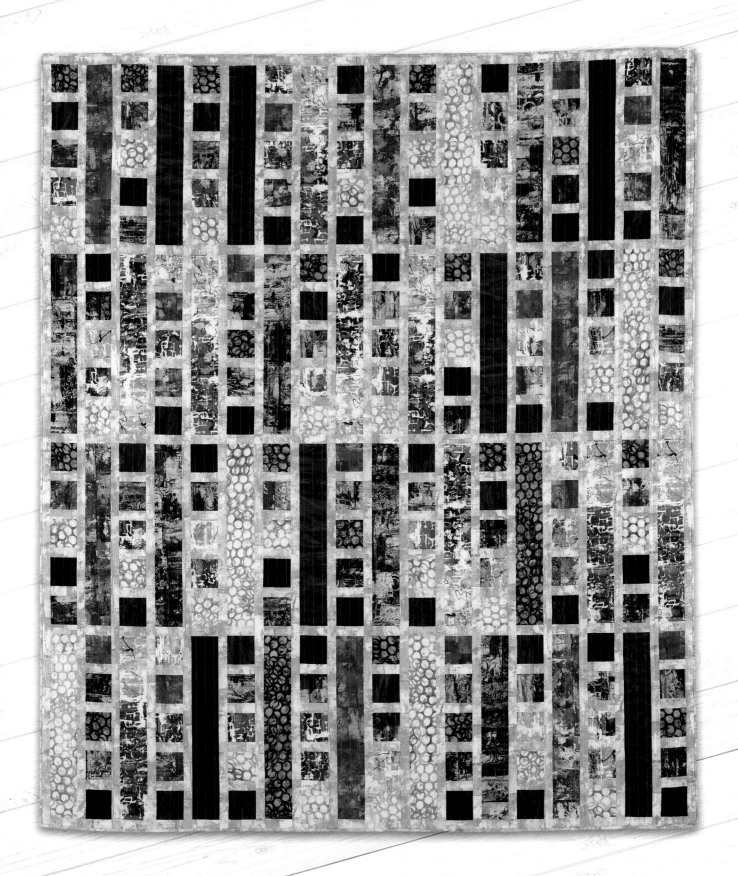

Block Assembly Instructions

1. Select fifteen (twenty, thirty, fifty-five) 3½" x 21" (8.89 x 53.34cm) strips from the fat quarters. Make sure to select strips from each fabric to create an even distribution throughout the final quilt.

2. Sew the 3½" x 21" (8.89 x 53.34cm) fat quarter strips to the 1½" x 21" (3.81 x 53.34cm) background strips along the long side to create fifteen (twenty, thirty, fifty-five) strip-pieced units that measure 4½" x 21" (11.43 x 53.34cm). Press the seams open.

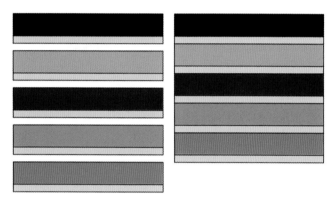

3. Select five strip-pieced units and sew them together along the long sides, placing the background fabric next to the fat quarter fabric as shown above. Press the seams open. The strip-pieced units should measure 20½" x 21" (52.07cm x 53.34cm).

Repeat to create three (four, six, eleven) strip-pieced units.

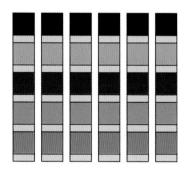

4. Cross-cut each strip-pieced unit into six 3½" x 20½" (8.89 x 52.07cm) Row A segments. Repeat with the remaining strip-pieced units to create a total of fourteen (twenty-three, thirty-six, sixty-three) Row A segments.

5. Select thirteen (twenty-two, thirty-six, sixty-two) 3½" x 21" (8.89 x 53.34cm) strips from the fat quarters. Trim them down to 3½" x 19" (8.89 x 48.26cm) rectangles.

6. Join the 3½" x 19½" (8.89 x 49.53cm) fat quarter rectangles with the 1½" x 3½" (3.81 x 8.89cm) background rectangles, sewing along the short sides. Press the seams open. Create a total of thirteen (twenty-two, thirty-six, sixty-two) Row B segments.

Quilt Assembly Instructions

1. Arrange the Row A and Row B segments in a layout that is pleasing to you according to the quilt layout diagram on page 81.

2. Join the segments into vertical rows.

3. Sew the vertical sashing background strips along the short sides in the following combinations:
- Crib: One 1½" x 40½" (3.81 x 102.87cm) strip and one 1½" x 20½" (3.81 x 52.07cm) strip per vertical row
- Throw: One 1½" x 40½" (3.81 x 102.87cm) strip and one 1½" x 20½" (3.81 x 52.07cm) strip per vertical row
- Full: Two 1½" x 40½" (3.81 x 102.87cm) strips per vertical row
- King: Two 1½" x 40½" (3.81 x 102.87cm) strips and one 1½" x 20½" (3.81 x 52.07cm) strip per vertical row

Press the seams open.

4. Sew the vertical sashing strips to the right side of each row. You will have one vertical sashing strip left over to sew to the left side of the first row. Press the seams open.

5. Join rows to complete the quilt top as shown in the quilt assembly diagram on page 80. Press all seams open.

6. Sew the top horizontal sashing background strips along the short sides to create one 1½" x 37½" (3.81 x 95.25cm) (61½" [1.56m], 73½" [1.87m], 101½" [2.58m]) sashing strip.

Press the seams open.

7. Sew the top horizontal sashing strip to the top of the quilt. Press the seam open.

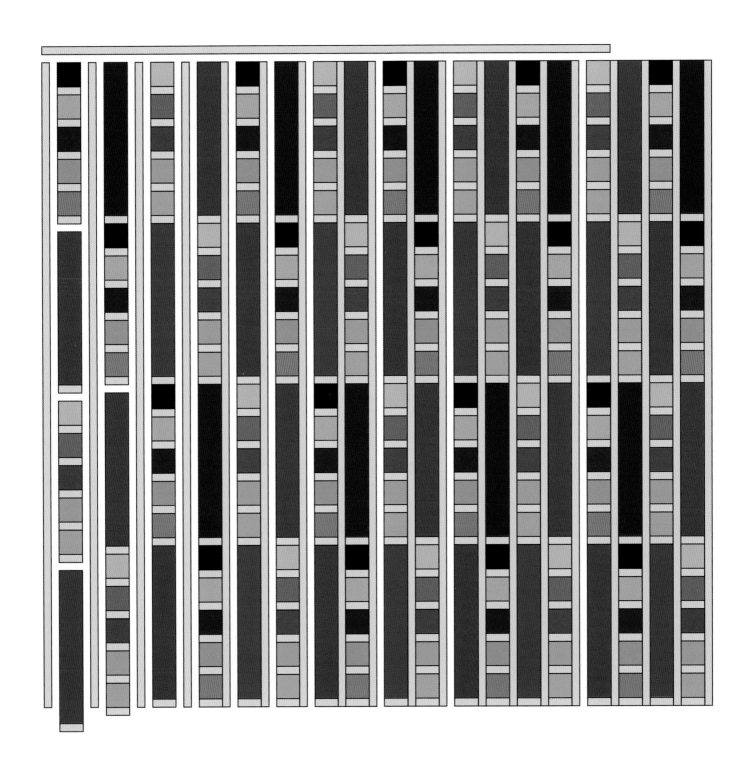

Quilt assembly diagram
(shown in Full size)

Crib   **Lap** **Full**   **King**

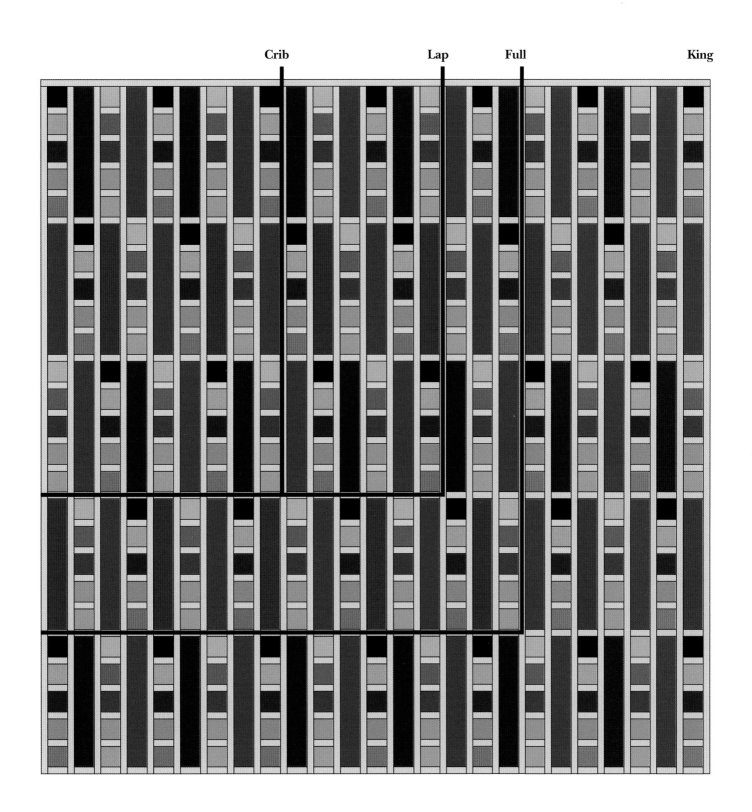

Quilt layout diagram

Sparkle

My idea for this quilt design changed completely right in the middle of sewing it together. I had planned to take my diamond blocks and turn them into smaller individual stars. I already had all my diamonds sewn together and was laying them out on my bed to work on the layout, but I quickly realized that it would make for a giant quilt that used a whole lot of background fabric. I changed gears and started making a large star that expanded out from the middle. I went from feeling OK about my design choice to absolutely loving it!

Like the fabric I used for Cross & Dot (page 44), this collection—Thistle Patch by Teresa Magnuson for Clothworks—was split pretty evenly into one-third light, one-third medium, and one-third dark fabrics. While that offers a lot of really great neutral options, it makes it challenging to design a quilt using all of the fabrics and still have clear contrast between the neutrals and the background. That challenge is solved in this quilt by using the light fabrics for the large diamond and the medium and dark prints for the smaller frame diamonds. The fabric placement creates the needed contrast between the block and the background and creates dimension as the star expands out.

Fun fact: The star block in Sparkle is exactly the same as the star block in Bling (page 38). So it just goes to show you how fabric and setting can completely transform the look of a quilt!

Fabric Requirements

	Fat Quarters	Background	Binding	Backing	Finished Size
Lap	8L, 10M/D	1¼ yards (1.14m)	⅔ yard (0.61m)	4⅓ yards (3.96m)	67½" x 69¾" (1.71 x 1.77m)

L = light, M = medium, D = dark

Cutting Instructions

You must use a 60-degree triangle ruler with all three points, like the Clearview Triangle, in order to cut the right number of diamonds and triangles for this pattern. The cutting instructions will not work if you use a 60-degree triangle ruler with one blunt point.

FAT QUARTERS

1. Select eight light fat quarters. Cut three 5" x 21" (12.70 x 53.34cm) strips from each.

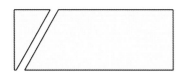

2. Select a 5" (12.70cm) strip. Using a 60-degree triangle ruler, line the 5" (12.70cm) line up with the bottom of the strip and line up the point even with the top of the strip. Cut the corner off the strip, leaving a 60-degree angle on the edge of the strip.

3. Flip the 60-degree ruler over so that the 5" (12.70cm) line is even with the top of the strip and the point is even with the bottom of the strip. The left side of the ruler should be even with the top left point you just cut. Cut along the right side of the ruler to create a 60-degree diamond.

Continue sliding the ruler down to cut three 5" (12.70cm) diamonds from each strip, for a total of nine 5" (12.70cm) diamonds from each fat quarter and a total of sixty-eight diamonds.

4. Select ten medium and dark fat quarters and cut six 2¾" x 21" (6.99 x 53.34cm) strips from each. Repeat Steps 1–3 with 2¾" x 21" (6.99 x 53.34cm) strips, cutting thirty-six 2¾" (6.99cm) diamonds from each fat quarter, for a total of 340 diamonds.

BACKGROUND

5. Cut five 7½" (19.05cm) x WOF strips. Select four strips, unfold the fabric, and arrange two strips on top of each other with wrong sides together. This will ensure that there are equal amounts of half-equilateral triangles.

6. Square up the left edge of the strips, cutting off the selvage edge. Then place the tip of the triangle ruler ¼" (0.64cm) from the bottom left of the strips, with the 7½" (19.05cm) mark even with the top of the strips. Cut along the left side of the ruler to create a half-equilateral triangle.

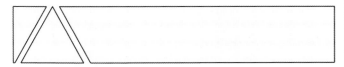

7. Flip the ruler so the tip is even with the top edge and the 7½" (19.05cm) mark is even with the bottom of the strips. Cut along the right side of the ruler to create an equilateral triangle.

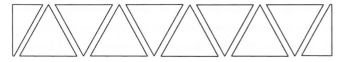

8. Continue in this manner until you have cut eight triangles and two half-equilateral triangles per strip.

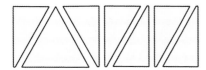

9. Select the remaining 7½" (19.05cm) x WOF strip. With the strip folded in half with the selvages together, follow the cutting layout above to cut two equilateral triangles and twelve half-equilateral triangles.

You will have a total of thirty-four equilateral triangles and twenty half-equilateral triangles.

BINDING

10. Cut eight 2½" (6.35cm) x WOF strips.

Block Assembly Instructions

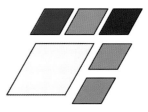

1. Select five 2¾" (6.99cm) diamonds and one 5" (12.70cm) diamond and arrange as shown above.

2. Place the small diamonds right sides together as shown above and sew a ¼" (0.64cm) seam. Press the seams open.

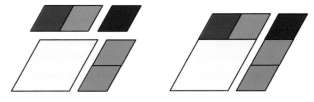

3. Join the top and bottom rows as shown above.

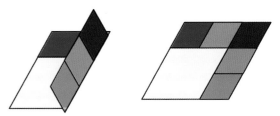

4. Sew the right row of small diamonds to the left row. Press seams open.

5. Repeat Steps 1–4 to make sixty-eight pieced diamonds.

Quilt Assembly Instructions

This quilt is actually quite easy. You will sew diamonds and triangles into a diagonal row. Then you will join the rows into a set of six wedges instead of traditional blocks. The wedges will be joined to complete the quilt top with no Y-seams.

1. Select two pieced diamonds from Step 5 of the Block Assembly Instructions.

2. Flip the upper diamond down so that when the right sides are together, the diamonds point in opposite directions, as seen above. The top points will stick out on either side about ¼" (0.64cm).

Your ¼" (0.64cm) seam line should be right in the valley where the points meet, as indicated by the red seam line above. Sew the diamonds together.

3. Press the seams open. This is the beginning of Wedge 1.

4. Use the numbered diagrams below to sew two of each wedge together by first sewing the diamonds, equilateral triangles, and half-equilateral triangles into rows and then sewing the rows together to make the wedge. Press all seams open.

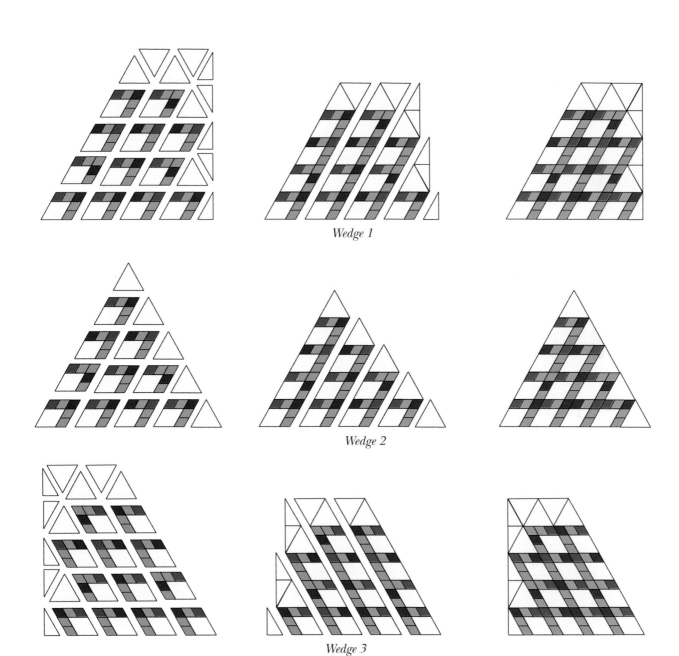

Wedge 1

Wedge 2

Wedge 3

5. Arrange the wedges as shown above.

6. Join Wedge 3 to Wedge 2. Press the seams open.

Quilt layout diagram

8. Join the quilt halves to complete the quilt top.

7. Join Wedge 1 to Wedge 2 to complete the quilt half. Press the seams open. Make two halves.

Stargazer

Quilted by Shelly Moore

I am not normally a fan of anything brown, but I couldn't resist Perennial by Sarah Golden for Andover Fabrics. I just loved the earthy hues with a modern twist. The block print flowers were also a big draw because I am almost as addicted to plants and gardening as I am to quilting.

For the design, I combined my all-time-favorite 60-degree triangle techniques to create a star that looked like six large petals with twelve small leaves surrounding the petals. The quilt has strip-pieced centers like in Lily Field (page 60), small diamonds, and an alternating setting like in Starburst, which is featured in my second book, *Fat Quarter Workshop: 12 Skill-Building Quilt Patterns*. The result is a fun, graphic modern star block.

When choosing what fabrics would go where, I chose my lightest prints for the strip-pieced center triangles to separate them from the background fabric. My darkest prints form the large equilateral triangles, and my medium prints are the small diamonds. A single solid neutral background gives the eye a place to rest, letting the fat quarter fabrics shine.

Fabric Requirements

	Fat Quarters	Background	Binding	Backing	# of blocks	Finished Size
Crib	4L, 4M, 4D	1¾ yards (1.60m)	⅔ yard (0.61m)	3½ yards (3.20m)	12	52½" x 66¾" (1.33 x 1.70m)
Full	7L, 7M, 7D	2½ yards (2.29m)	⅔ yard (0.61m)	5¼ yards (4.80m)	20	70" x 82⅛" (1.78 x 2.09m)
Queen	9L, 9M, 9D	3 yards (2.74m)	¾ yard (0.69m)	7¾ yards (7.09m)	25	87½" x 82⅛" (2.22 x 2.09m)
King	12L, 12M, 12D	4 yards (3.66m)	1 yard (0.91m)	9¼ yards (8.46m)	36	105" x 97¾" (2.67 x 2.48m)

L = light, M = medium, D = dark

Cutting Instructions

You must use a 60-degree triangle ruler with all three points, like the Clearview Triangle, in order to cut the right amount of diamonds and triangles for this pattern. The cutting instructions will not work if you use a 60-degree triangle ruler with one blunt point.

LIGHT FAT QUARTERS

1. From each light fat quarter, cut six 2⅞" x 21½" (7.30 x 54.61cm) strips, for a total of twenty-four (forty, fifty, seventy-two) strips. Set aside for block assembly.

MEDIUM FAT QUARTERS

2. From each medium fat quarter, cut six 2¾" x 21½" (6.99 x 54.61cm) strips, for a total of twenty-four (forty, fifty, seventy-two) strips.

Using a 60-degree triangle ruler, line the 2¾" (6.99cm) line up with the bottom of the strip and line up the point even with the top of the strip. Cut the corner off the strip, leaving a 60-degree angle on the edge of the strip. Discard the corner.

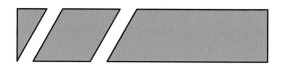

88

Flip the 60-degree ruler over so that the 2¾" (6.99cm) line is even with the top of the strip and the point is even with the bottom of the strip. The left side of the ruler should be even with the top left point you just cut. Cut along the right side of the ruler to create a 60-degree diamond.

Continue sliding the ruler down to cut six 2¾" (6.99cm) diamonds from each strip, for a total of 144 (240, 300, 432) diamonds.

DARK FAT QUARTERS

3. From each dark fat quarter, cut three 5¼" x 21½" (13.34 x 54.61cm) strips, for a total of twelve (twenty, twenty-five, thirty-six) strips.

Using a 60-degree triangle ruler, line the 5¼" (13.34cm) line up with the bottom of the strip and line up the point even with the top of the strip. Cut the corner off the strip on the left side of the ruler, leaving a 60-degree angle on the edge of the strip. Discard the corner. Cut along the right side of the ruler to create a 60-degree triangle.

Flip the 60-degree ruler over so that the 5¼" (13.34cm) line is even with the top of the strip and the point is even with the bottom of the strip. The left side of the ruler should be even with the edge you just cut. Cut along the right side of the ruler to create another 60-degree triangle.

Continue sliding the ruler down to cut six 5¼" (13.34cm) diamonds from each strip, for a total of seventy-two (120, 150, 216) triangles.

BACKGROUND

4. Cut fourteen (twenty-two, twenty-eight, forty) 3" (7.62cm) x WOF strips. From each strip, cut twenty-two 60-degree triangles, using the same technique as in Step 3, for a total of 288 (480, 600, 864) triangles.

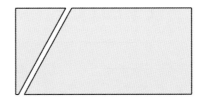

5. Cut one (two, two, two) 9½" (24.13cm) x WOF strips. Leave the strips folded in half with the selvages together for cutting. Square up the edges by cutting off the selvages. For the rest of the cutting instructions, you will need to use a 6" x 24" (15.24 x 60.96cm) ruler with a 60-degree line.

Make a mark at the bottom of the strip, ¼" (0.64cm) from the squared edges. Line the 60-degree line of your ruler up with the bottom of the strip and the mark so that the ruler crosses the strip of fabric.

Cut to create a half-equilateral triangle with a ¼" (0.64cm) seam past the center for your seam allowance.

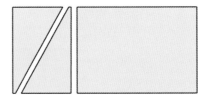

Line your ruler up across the fabric strip, ¼" (0.64cm) to the right of the point you just cut. Cut to create a half-equilateral triangle with a ¼" (0.64cm) seam past the center.

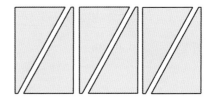

Repeat to cut the remainder of the strip. Your strip will look like the diagram above when you are finished, but because the strip was folded over, you will have twelve mirror-image half-equilateral triangles per strip to be used as setting triangles.

You will need twelve (sixteen, twenty, twenty-four) setting triangles.

BINDING

6. Cut seven (eight, nine, eleven) 2½" (6.35cm) x WOF strips.

Block Assembly Instructions

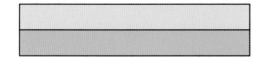

1. Select light strips and sew them together on the long side. Press the seams open. Strip sets should measure 5¼" x 21½" (13.34 x 54.61cm).

Repeat to create twelve (twenty, twenty-five, thirty-six) strip sets. If you want to have six matching diamonds for the inner blocks, sew six (ten, thirteen, eighteen) sets of two matching strip sets.

2. Using an equilateral triangle ruler, cut six 60-degree triangles from each strip set, using the same technique as in Cutting Instructions Step 3. You will have a total of seventy-two (120, 150, 216) pieced equilateral triangles for the block centers, or twelve (twenty, twenty-five, thirty-six) matching sets of six.

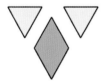

3. Select twelve matching 2¾" (6.99cm) diamonds and stack them up. Then select twenty-four 3" (7.62cm) background triangles and arrange them in equal stacks on either side of the 2¾" (6.99cm) diamonds as shown above.

4. Place a left background triangle right sides together with a diamond. The top points will align, and the bottom left point will extend beyond the diamond. Sew together with a ¼" (0.64cm) seam. Press the seams open.

Next, sew a background triangle to the right side of the diamond to create twelve matching pieced 60-degree triangles as shown above. The triangles should be 5¼" (13.34cm) tall.

Repeat to create 144 (240, 300, 432) pieced triangles, or twelve (twenty, twenty-five, thirty-six) matching sets of twenty-four.

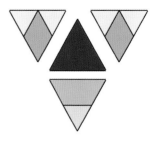

5. Select twelve matching pieced triangles from Step 3, six matching strip-pieced triangles from Step 2, and six matching triangles from Cutting Instructions Step 3. Stack them up and arrange as shown above.

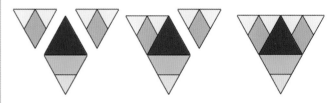

6. Join the triangles from Step 2 and Cutting Instructions Step 3. Press the seams open.

Following the same process as in Step 4, sew the pieced triangles from Step 3 to the sides of the diamond to create six pieced triangles as shown above. Press the seams open.

7. Arrange three pieced triangles from Step 6 as shown above.

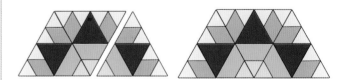

Matching the seams, sew the left and right triangles to the center triangle one at a time. Press the seams open.

Repeat with the remaining three pieced triangles from Step 6 to make the second half of the block. *Do not* sew the blocks together.

Repeat to make twenty-four (forty, fifty, seventy-two) block halves, or twelve (twenty, twenty-five, thirty-six) matched sets of two block halves.

Quilt Assembly Instructions

1. Arrange the block halves into a quilt design that is pleasing to you according to the quilt assembly diagram below. Place the setting triangles from Cutting Instructions Step 5 at the top and bottom of the rows.

   Note that there will be setting triangles at the top and bottom of every row for all sizes, but the quilt layout diagram on the facing page shows them only on the King-sized version.

2. Sew the block halves into vertical rows, then join the vertical rows to complete the quilt top.

Quilt assembly diagram
(shown in Full size)

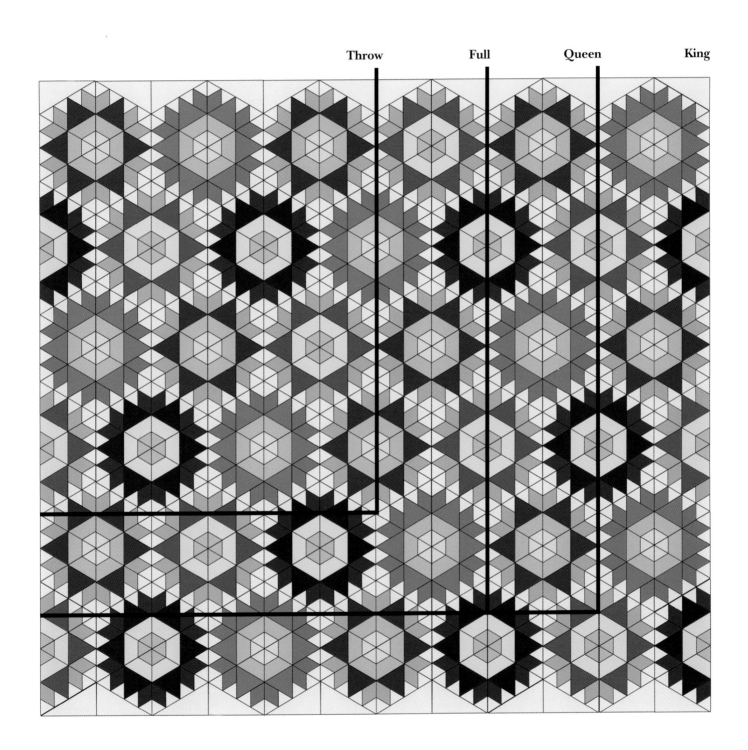

Quilt layout diagram

Index

Acknowledgments

I designed the quilts in this book between the fall of 2019 and the spring of 2021. In the fall of 2019, I was *very* pregnant with my second daughter and working a reduced schedule due to the extra monitoring required for a geriatric pregnancy. (Side note: I was due two days after my thirty-fifth birthday—we really need a better term for pregnancies in women over thirty-five!) My daughter arrived in January 2020, two days before my birthday and right before the world went crazy. I spent most of 2020 and the beginning of 2021 going between my house and my shop with a baby, a six-year-old, and a Basset Hound puppy named Jellyroll in tow.

These quilts and this book would not have been possible without my fabulous team at Quilt Addicts Anonymous. They make me look good every day, and they really went above and beyond as we figured out new ways to work and be safe. And, thanks to them, I only had to bind one of the quilts in this book!

Another big thank you to my longarmer, Shelly Moore, who quilted nearly half of these quilts both to help reduce my workload during the pregnancy and then to help me meet this book deadline while running a business and constantly having two children around with no in-person school or daycare. She always does a fabulous job and helps bring my tops to life.

Lastly, thank you to my husband, who is an equal partner in business, parenting, and life. I wouldn't want to be quarantined with anyone but you and our little family.

About the Author

Growing up, Stephanie Soebbing had one goal: to make a career out of writing. Really, she just wanted to be creative, but it took some time to figure that out. She started her career as a journalist and then moved into digital marketing.

While she was pregnant with her first child, Stephanie was looking for a way out of the rat race of the advertising world so she could have more flexibility to be with her daughter.

That "way out" came when she first started teaching students her first Block of the Month design at her local quilt shop. She published her pattern online and combined her marketing, story-telling, and video production training from her journalism days into her blog, *QuiltAddictsAnonymous.com*. It became a fast-growing pattern design company and online fabric store.

Seven years later, those first students have turned into thousands of quilters worldwide who have been inspired by Stephanie's designs and video tutorials. Today she works with her husband at their online quilt shop, Quilt Addicts Anonymous, in Rock Island, Illinois.

You can find more of Stephanie's original patterns at *shop.QuiltAddictsAnonymous.com* and browse hundreds of free quilting tutorials at *QuiltAddictsAnonymous.com/tutorials*.